TASSELS & TRIMMINGS

TASSELS & TRIMMINGS

Providing the Finishing Touches

by

EFFIE MITROFANIS

Add a tassel to it!

Effie Mitrofanis

10/11/92

SIMON & SCHUSTER
AUSTRALIA

TASSELS AND TRIMMINGS

First Published in Australia 1992 by
Simon & Schuster Australia
20 Barcoo Street, East Roseville, NSW 2069

A Paramount Communications Company
Sydney, New York, London, Toronto,
Tokyo, Singapore.

Conceived, designed and produced for the publishers by
J.M.McGregor Pty. Ltd., P.O. Box 6990
Gold Coast Mail Centre, Qld 4217

National Library of Australia
Cataloguing in Publication data

Mitrofanis, Effie.
Tassels and Trimmings

Includes index
ISBN 0 7318 0022 2

1. Tassels. 2. Needlework. 1. Title.
746.27

Designed and Typeset by Glenn Ray
Photography by Lee Sincic
Diagrams by John Sarafoudis

Printed in Hong Kong by South China Printing Co (1988) Ltd

Contents

ACKNOWLEDGEMENTS

My grateful thanks to DMC Australia, Thorobred Yarns and Bernina Australia.

Sincere thanks to: my fellow tutors at the Embroiderers' Guild NSW, namely Karma Victoria Bains, Heather Joynes, Patricia Langford, Janice Rawlinson and Alison Snepp, and to my friends Robyn Hayden, Joan Jefferies and Eileen Gale for the loan of their unique tassels shown in this book; to my brother-in-law Emanouel Zouroudis for the loan of his late mother's needlelace and crochet work; Anna Thomson of Narrabri, NSW for supplying Australian cotton bolls; Frances Fleming of Lintrathen by Kirriemuir, Angus, Scotland for her own handspun wool; Australian handspun wool from Tenterfield, NSW.

Special thanks to photographer Lee Sincic for his assistance, expertise and meticulous attention to detail.

Special thanks to my dear friend Eileen Gale for her encouragement, computer assistance, indexing and proofreading the final manuscript.

My very special thanks to my husband Memo and my daughters Helen and Maria for their encouragement, patience and forbearance not only during the writing of this book but all the other times when embroidery has preoccupied me.

Introduction

Passementerie is a French word for which there is no exact English equivalent. *Trimmings* is the closest in meaning and includes tassels, fringes and braids. Trimmings probably started from the need to finish off warp threads on the end of weaving by knotting them to prevent unravelling. These formed fringes and soon fringes were made for their own sake to sew or nail onto upholstered furniture and furnishings such as cushions, bed hangings, curtains and chairs. They were used to cover seams, as insertions and edgings. Usually the upholsterer sold the trimmings along with his other goods and it was he who decided on and provided the correct trimmings for his finished handwork – a very specialised craft.

Trimmings were used extensively from the 17th to the early 19th century on upholstered items adding colour and richness.

Master trimming makers used intricate looms designed for different types of trim and these looms involved complex arrangements of wheels and bobbins and a wide variety of specialised implements. Finishing was a tedious job carried out by female piece workers for low wages.

Tassels using moulds are masterpieces of intricate, three dimensional construction where creative inventiveness is employed to cover the joins in decorative concealment.

Few examples of these very rich articles remain as their weight caused them to become damaged or lost. Because of the expense due to the long hard labour required to produce them, they generally were not replaced.

The most popular and romantic trimming is a tassel simply defined as a bunch of threads tied together. It is hard to imagine this definition adequately describing the beauty and fascination which tassels have evoked since the beginning of human existence. A tassel can also be described as 'an ornamental tuft of threads or cords of equal length, hanging loosely from a knot or something resembling this - as a tuft of corn silk'.

Tassels have many and varied practical and decorative uses. Some practical uses are tassels on the end of bell pulls, old fashioned light switch cords, keys and on the end of zippers. Nothing is quite as decorative as tassels – on clothing, furniture, soft furnishings, cushions, curtains, lamps, hats, hair ornaments, earrings, bags, boxes, bookmarks, letter openers, door and drawer knobs, scissors and military accoutrements. Tassels are also used as animal trappings - on sacred cows, on horses and as false eyelashes for camels.

In the Middle East a row of tassels known as false eyelashes was used to cover camels' eyes to protect them from the dust of desert skirmishes. Nowadays they are only used for parades.

Tassels have many moods and personalities - rich and exotic Arabian nomadic tribal tent homes; Egyptian princesses and temples; soft Greek maidens; earthy African tribal costume; American Indian dress; the mysterious Orient; the opulent French court of the 18th century; formal English drawing rooms; middle European peasant costume; Victorian door curtains. Tassels attached to braid in geometric arrangements decorate Orthodox church vestments. A most formidable tassel is the Scottish sporran and bagpipe tails.

Nature abounds in inspirations for creative tassels - shells, flowers, leaves, gum blossoms and fungi.

As well as being a bunch of threads tied together, tassels need to be pendulous, hanging and free and may be made from many different materials. Any kind of yarn, thread, ribbon, torn strips of fabric, rouleaux, leather thonging, unravelled fabric threads, cords, feathers, felt, braids and beads can be used to create this decorative hanging bauble.

A great variety of cords can be made to hold the tassel or tassels and instructions for some of them are given in Chapter 3.

Chapter 1 shows the materials, yarns and equipment needed to make tassels and trimmings. It also shows how to make, step by step, a variety of tassels from a simple basic tassel to more elaborate ones. Chapter 2 gives details of how to create rich, exotic tassels, decorative special effects and the use of padding and foundations. Chapter 4 gives instructions for a variety of fringes. Chapter 5 details useful and decorative knots and Chapter 6 practical and decorative stitchery.

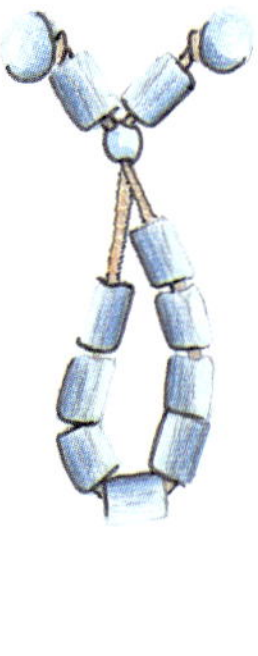

Chapter 1

Materials, Yarns and Equipment

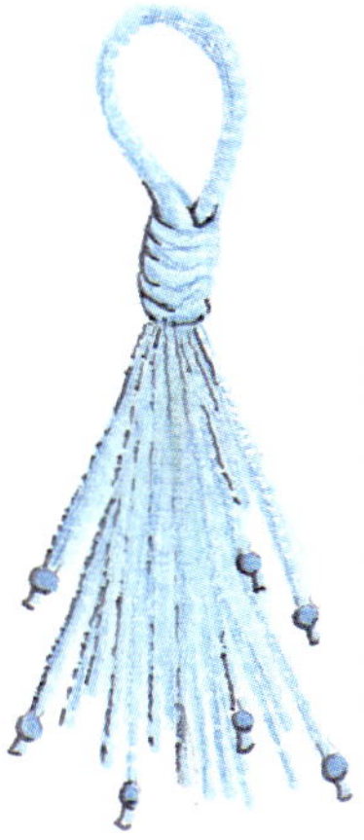

Materials and Yarns

The material chosen creates the whole personality of the tassel. Thicker woollen yarn makes up into a chunky, warm tassel which can be plump and cuddly or long and slender. Knitting and crochet yarns offer a very wide range of thickness and texture while embroidery threads offer a large selection of colours and finish. Different results are achieved when using shiny coton perle, fine silk, metallic, rayon or stranded embroidery floss than matt threads such as crochet cotton or string. Generally speaking any yarn may be used to make tassels. In addition hand or machine made cords, ribbons, metallics, twine, torn or cut strips of fabric, and leather strips make up into attractive tassels. Large beads of any shape or size may be used for padding as well as decorating the tassel and its cord.

Equipment

One of the advantages of tasselmaking is that it requires very little equipment:-

- Thick card around which to wind yarn.
- Scissors: A sharp pair of embroidery scissors, larger fabric scissors and scissors for cutting paper and card.
- Needles: Knitter's needles also known as bodkins or rug needles with a very large eye for threading thick cord. Assorted sizes of tapestry needles with dull points for generally sewing the tassel – these don't split the yarn which sharps tend to do.
  Assorted sharps, crewel and beading needles to be used for decorating the tassel.
  A needle available from specialty embroidery shops is called *Pace's Big Eye Needle* which is a fine, easy threading sewing needle for thick yarn and cording.
- Sewing machine.

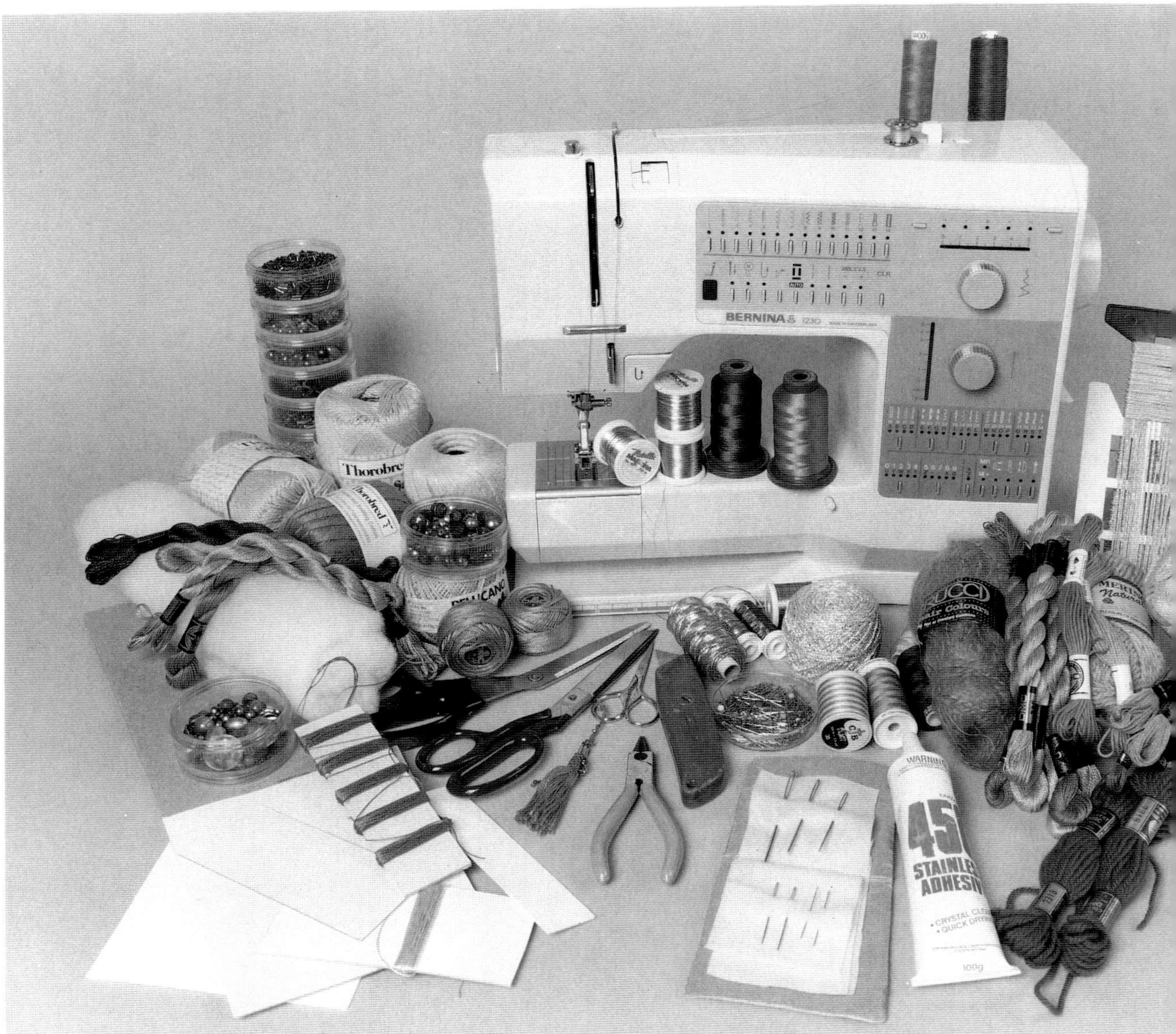

Materials, Yarns and Equipment

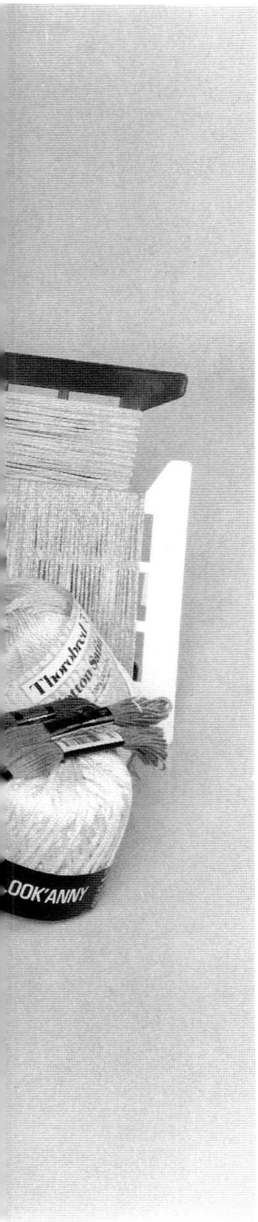

Reference is made to other materials in Chapter 2 - Decorative Special Effects.Commercially made tassels for trimming curtains and furnishings are made around a wooden mould with a hole down the centre. These moulds are usually made especially for the manufacturer and aren't generally sold in retail stores.

Chapter 2 gives full instructions on how to create your own moulds and padding techniques for making sculptured shapes. These include pieces of quilt wadding, rolled felt and beads which may be used as foundations to make the tassel bigger or to take on a particular shape.

A sewing machine makes quick, attractive cords and rouleaux as shown in Chapter 3.

Where to begin

As every tassel in this book is a project in itself someone just starting out to make a tassel could well be confused about what to do first.
I suggest that the first project for a beginner would be a basic tassel. Look around your home for any item which might be enhanced or revamped by adding tassels, referring also to the list of uses below.

Choose matching or contrasting colours and yarns and make one or more basic tassels. When you feel comfortable with the basic tassel start decorating the head by trying out any of the methods described in Chapter 1.

When you feel more adventurous play around with the decorative and special effects in Chapter 2.

List of uses

Tassels may be used to trim the following:-

Bags; bookmarks; boxes; cake decorating; chatelaines; child's toys; clothing; cords; curtain tie-backs; cushions; cylinders and jewel boxes; door and window curtains; fan trimmings; fresh and dried flower arrangements; gift wrapping; hats; keys; lampshades and light fittings; mobiles; pens and pencils; purses; reticules; scissors; unisex pouches; utility-tote-work bags; window blinds.

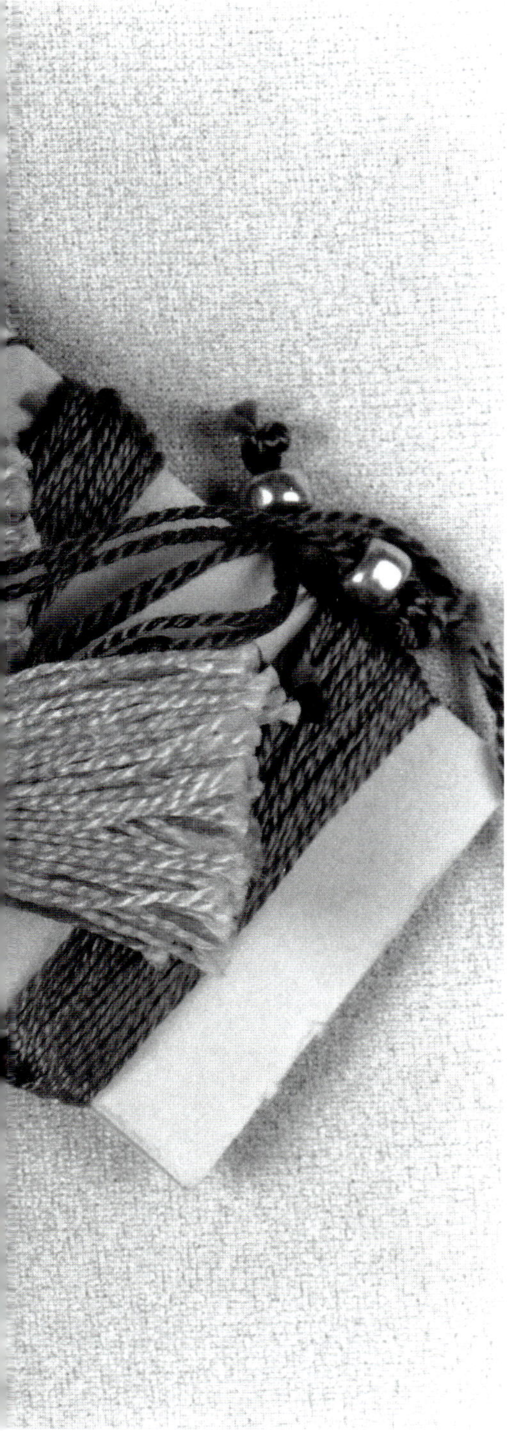

Basic Tasselmaking

Definition of terms

Tassels are described by various terms referring to their elemental structure.

Cord is a length of yarn either plain or decorative which ties, holds together and is used to attach the tassel.

Head is that part of the tassel above the neck.

Neck is the tied and knotted part of the tassel which holds the yarn intact and separates the head from the skirt.

Skirt is the yarn which hangs below the neck of the tassel. A great variety of tassels can be achieved by altering any of the above elements.

Scale means the size of the tassel. This differs depending on the length of the tassel, the thickness of yarn, and the number of times the yarn is wound around a card pattern.

Card pattern is a piece of firm cardboard cut to a desired measurement around which the yarn is wound to form the head and skirt of the tassel, refer photo page 12.

Knots are used to tie the tassel. Refer to Chapter 5 for instructions.

Basic Tassels, braid and mass production (also Plate I) – on the left two purchased braids have been machine zigzag stitched together and a Basic Tassel No. 1 attached to the braid. A card template shows the mass production method and two Basic Tassels No. 1 have been tied with contrasting yarn over the wrapped neck.

General Instructions

The procedure for making tassels is to:-

1. Determine the length and scale.
2. Cut out a rectangular card pattern of the desired length and a practical width for handling.
3. Wind the chosen yarn round and round the card pattern starting and finishing the yarn at the bottom of the card.
4. Cut a length of the same or contrasting yarn about 45 cm (18 in) long and pass it under the wound yarn at the top of the tassel, tying it with a firm reef knot.
5. Take the circle of yarn off the card pattern; do not cut the end at this stage.
6. Cut another length of yarn approximately 20 cm (8 in) long and tie it around the tassel using a reef knot or double tie and wrap knot at the neck of the tassel. Let the ties blend with the threads of the tassel skirt and trim any excess.
7. With a sharp pair of scissors cut the bottom loop of the tassel to trim.

Making Basic Tassels

The number of times the yarn is wound around the card pattern depends on the length of the tassel, the thickness and weight of yarn and your own preference.

In the following instructions some measurements are given for card pattern sizes and approximate numbers of times the yarn is wound to produce the author's tassels. These measurements are given as a starting point and should the size and scale not suit your requirements you may vary the yarn and measurements. It is advisable to keep a notebook handy when making tassels to record measurements, yarn and results to save time and trouble in the future.

Basic Tassel No. 1 - wrapped neck – Photo page 12 and Plate I

1. Wind yarn around card pattern 4 cm (1.5 in) wide approximately seventy-five times using equivalent to No. 8 coton perle or crochet cotton - requires approximately 7 m (7.75 yds) of yarn - or fifty times using equivalent No. 5 coton perle - requires approximately 5 m (5.5 yds).
2. While the yarn is still on the card cut a separate length of 46 cm (18in) yarn or cord, double it, and thread it through the top and tie a firm reef knot to hold the yarn together.

3. Remove the wound yarn from the card - this is made easier by bending the card slightly.

4. Tie the tassel at the neck with a length of yarn 60 cm (24 in) long with a reef knot or a double tie and wrap knot.

5. Trim the skirt or leave it looped.

The head of this tassel may be seen to be flat so that its head has a front and a back instead of a spherical or ball shape. Although this is a very simple basic tassel it is very attractive used on its own, in bunches, or secured by stitching to ribbon or braid at intervals as a fringed trimming. An overhand knot tied on the holding cord approximately 4 cm (1.5 in) above the top of the tassel makes an attractive finish.

Basic Tassel No. 2 – Photo page 12 and Plate I

This tassel differs from Basic Tassel No. 1 in that the neck is not wrapped but simply tied ready for embellishment or variations.

1. Wind yarn around 7 cm (2.75 in) card pattern approximately one hundred times for No. 8 coton perle equivalent or seventy-five times for No. 5 coton perle equivalent.
2. Wind the thread round and round the card pattern starting and finishing the thread at the bottom of the card. Note: when winding the yarn around the card, build up the yarn on top of itself at the top of the tassel head so that it is as narrow as possible. This makes it easier to proceed to the next step.
3. Cut a length of the same or contrasting yarn about 45 cm (18 in) long and thread it with a needle under the wound yarn at the top of the tassel, tying it with a reef knot.
4. Take the circle of yarn off the card pattern - this is made easier by bending the card slightly - do not cut the end at this stage.
5. Cut another length of thread approximately 20 cm (8 in) long and tie it around the threads once or twice finishing off with a reef knot to form the neck.
6. Let the tails of yarn blend with the threads of the tassel skirt and trim any excess.

The tassel head is now ready to be embellished.

Mass production – Photo page 12 and Plate I

1. A quick way to produce many basic tassels of the same size is to cut out a card pattern approximately 30.5 cm (12 in) long and as wide as the required length of the tassel.

2. Wind yarn around the card at one end to form the first tassel.

3. Take the yarn, without cutting it, approximately 2.5 cm (1 in) along the card and start winding another tassel.
4. Continue in this manner until the card is full.
5. Tie the tops of the tassels as set out in Basic Tassel Nos. 1 and 2.
6. Remove tassels from the card, cutting the joining yarn, then tying the necks of each tassel.

Strings of tassels for braiding

a) Work steps 1 to 4 above, mass production.

b) Thread a length of yarn in a tapestry or knitter's needle.

c) While the tassels are still on the card take the yarn from one tassel to another tying the tops with two or three detached buttonhole stitches.

d) Should you wish to make a cord between each tassel work knotted or braided finger cord.

e) Remove the tassels one by one from the card to tie each neck in place. Cut the joining yarn between tassels.

f) Attach to ribbon or cord with hand or machine stitching.

Method 1 - Detached buttonhole starting at the neck. – Plate II and Photo page 22

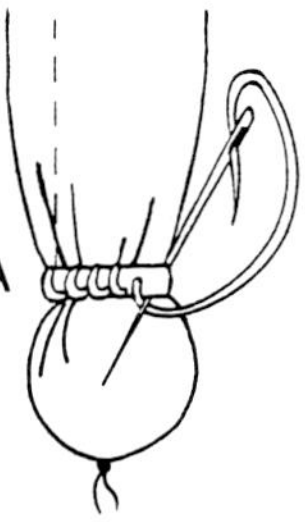

Fig. 1a

1. Make Basic Tassel No. 1 or 2.
2. Thread a very long piece of yarn approximately 1 to 1.5 m (5 ft) through a tapestry needle and take the needle and yarn up through the centre of the tassel skirt, leaving the tail of yarn hanging loose to blend with the other yarns in the skirt.
3. Bring the needle out at a point just above the neck at A. Refer to Figure 1a.
4. With the tassel skirt held away from you and the head towards you start making the first row of approximately eight to ten detached buttonhole stitches evenly around the tied thread of the neck. More detached buttonhole stitches around the neck will result in a closer mesh covering the head of the tassel while fewer stitches result in a more open mesh. Changing tension from tight, medium or loose also changes the effect. Refer to Figure 1b.

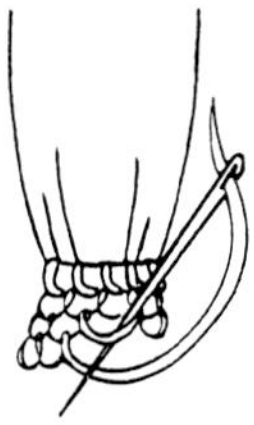

Fig. 1b

5. Continue detached buttonhole stitching into the loops of the first row spiralling up towards the top of the head. Do not decrease stitches as you approach the top but tighten the tension of each stitch until the gap at the top closes.

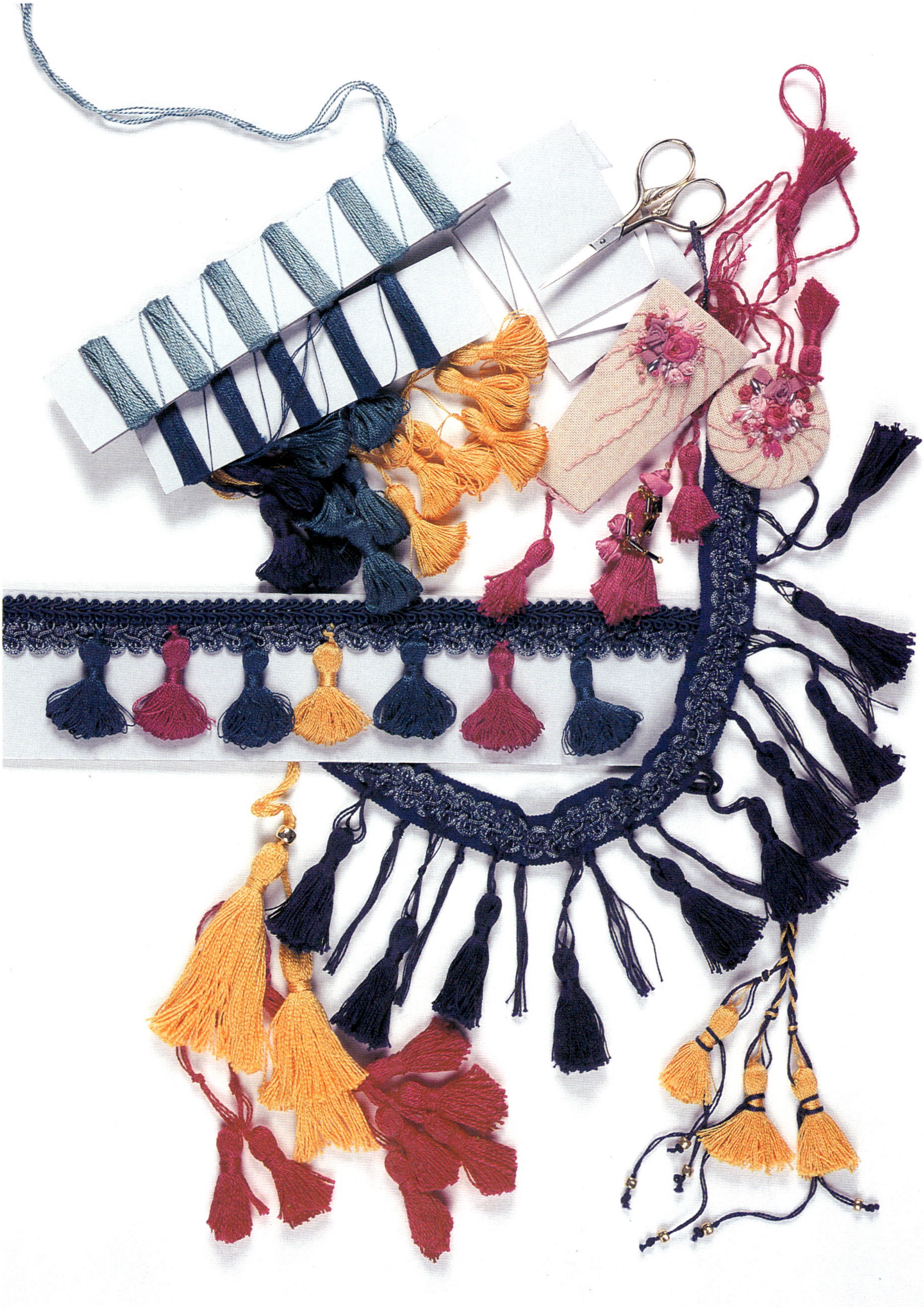

Plate I

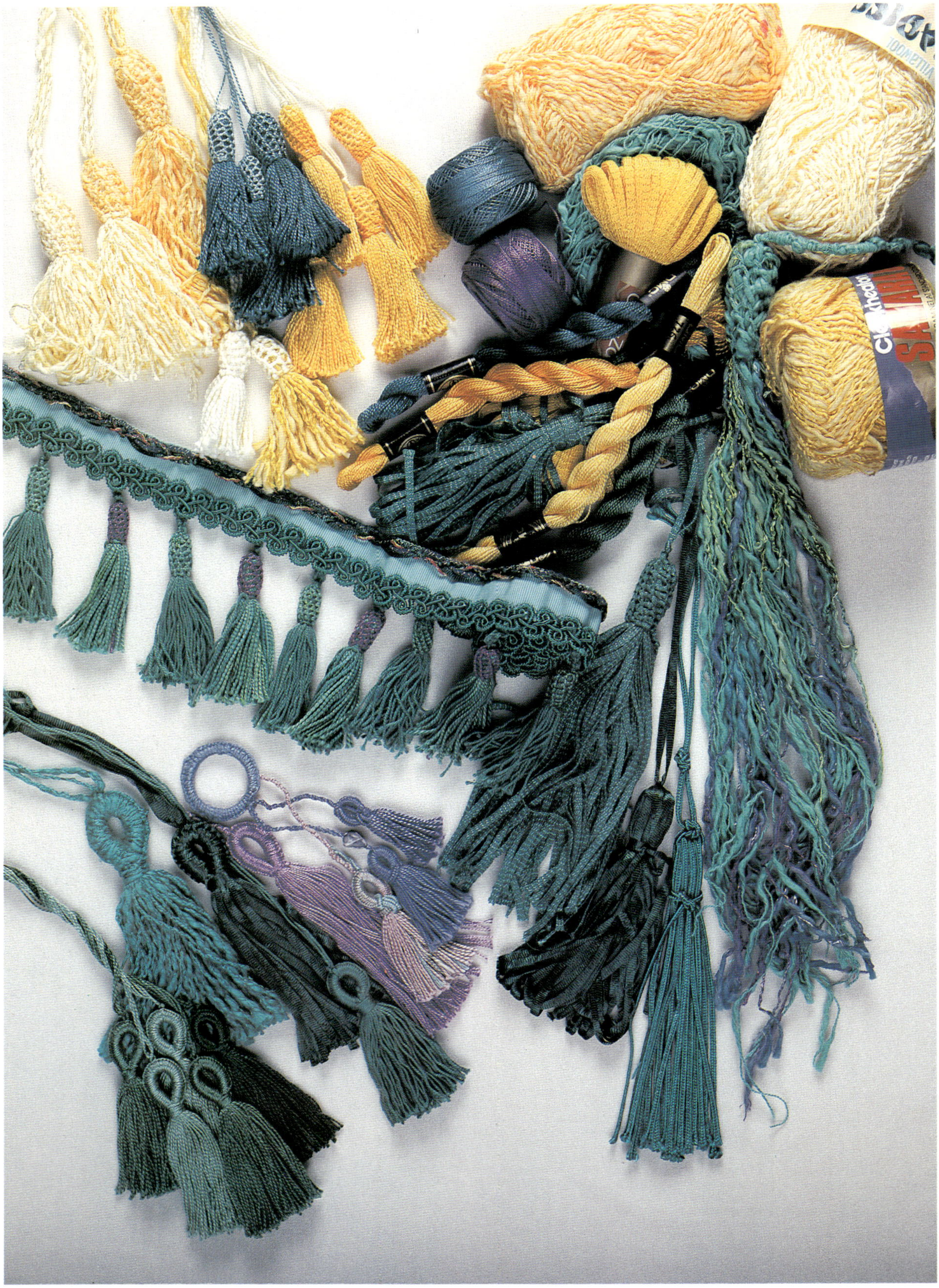

Plate II

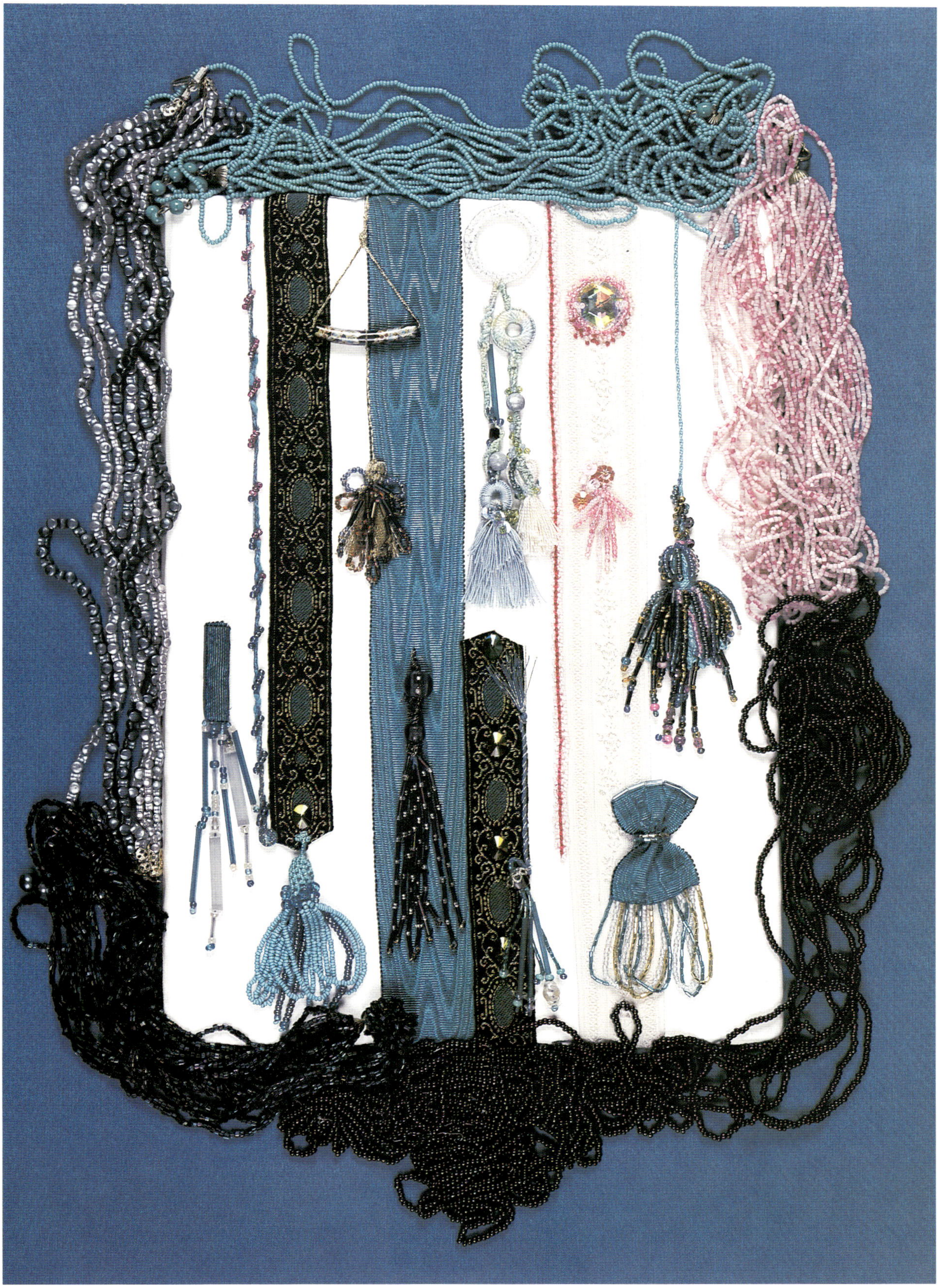

Plate III

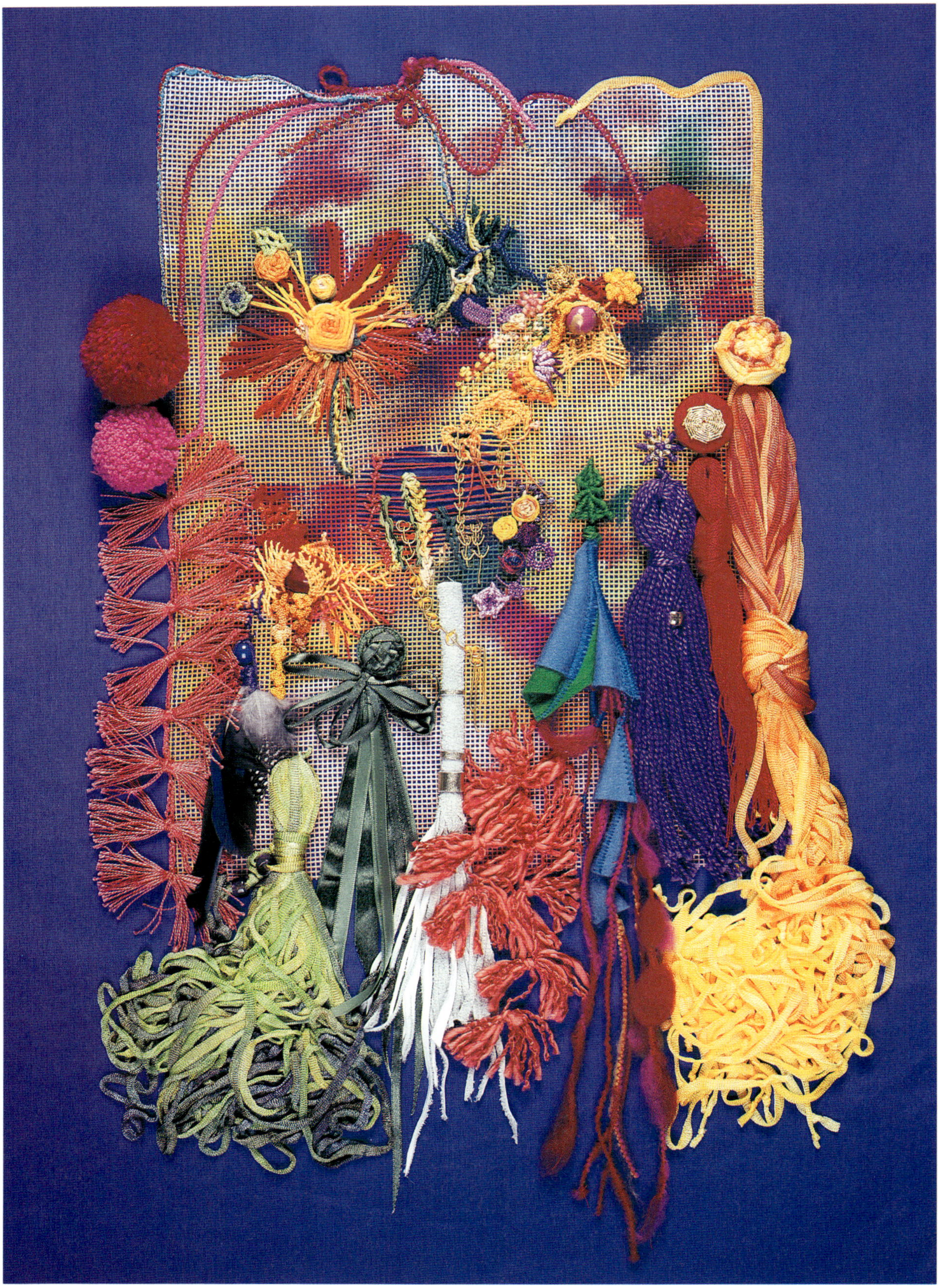

Plate IV

Plate I Basic Tassel No. 1

Top left: Card templates wrapped with yarn to mass produce tassels. Centre: Two types of purchased braid zigzag stitched by machine with tassels left looped. The other braid is purchased braid machine stitched to grosgrain ribbon. Tassels have been attached with hand stitching and alternate with overhand knot tassels. These fringed braids may be used to decorate curtains, furnishings, cushions, hats, clothing and any other project requiring a fringe. The skirts of some of the tassels have been cut in a V shape, some have been left looped and others decorated with beads and ribbon roses. Bottom right: Three tassels have been tied at the neck in a contrasting colour with beads threaded to the tails and secured with overhand knots. A second, decorative holding cord has been threaded through the top head of the tassel.

Plate II Detached buttonhole heads

Examples of Basic Tassel No. 2 and detached buttonhole head. The braid holding the tassels is made from a three strand plaited braid combining machine made cords and a purchased braid machine stitched to a grosgrain ribbon.

Plate III Beads

Various types of tassels using beads and ribbon. The stitch worked alongside the white flowered ribbon is Pekinese stitch.

Plate IV Garden of Tassels and Woven Webs.

1. Machine made cords
2. Method 11 pom poms
3. Stem stitch webs
4. Needle weaving
5. Back stitch webs
6. Cretan stitch webs
7. Raised chain band
8. Head back stitch web
9. Stem stitch web
10. Woven web stitch plain weave
11. Leather method 12
12. Flat knot method 10
13. Overhand knot method 9
14. Feathers method 15
15. Horizontal wrapped neck method 16
16. Fringed tassel
17. Felt method 14
18. Ribbon method 13 with head made of two detached buttonholed metal washers sewn together then embroidered with a woven web.

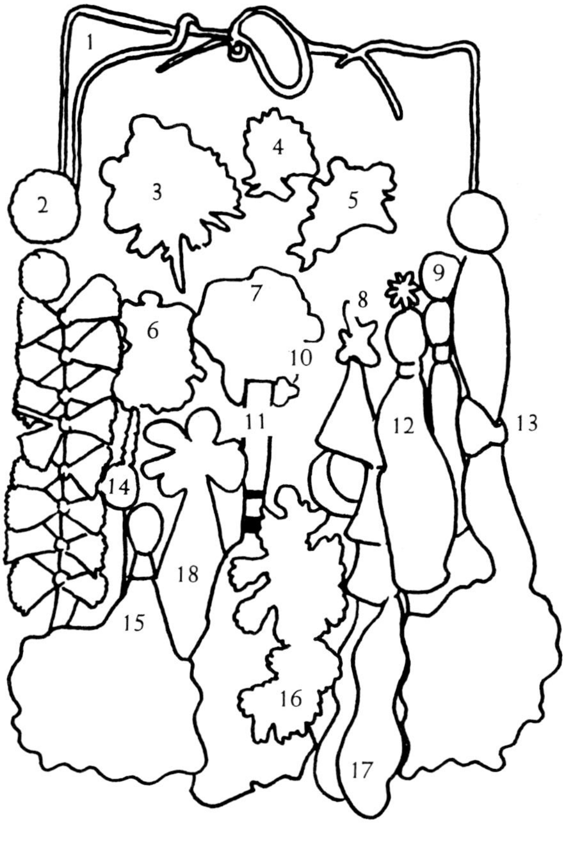

Method 2 - Detached buttonhole head starting at the top – Plate II, Photo below and Figure 2

Almost the same result is achieved with method 2 as method 1. Until you are familiar with this procedure I suggest that you use a heavier yarn of a different colour from the yarn in the body of the tassel to work detached buttonhole over the head.

1. Make Basic Tassel No. 1 or 2.
2. Cut a very long piece of yarn approximately 1 to 1.5 m (5 ft) and thread it into a tapestry needle as it is best if the tassel head is embroidered without starting a new thread in the process. If you do run out of yarn refer to next page, 'running out of yarn'.
3. Take the needle and yarn up through the centre of the tassel skirt and head, leaving the tail of yarn hanging loose to blend with the other yarns in the skirt.

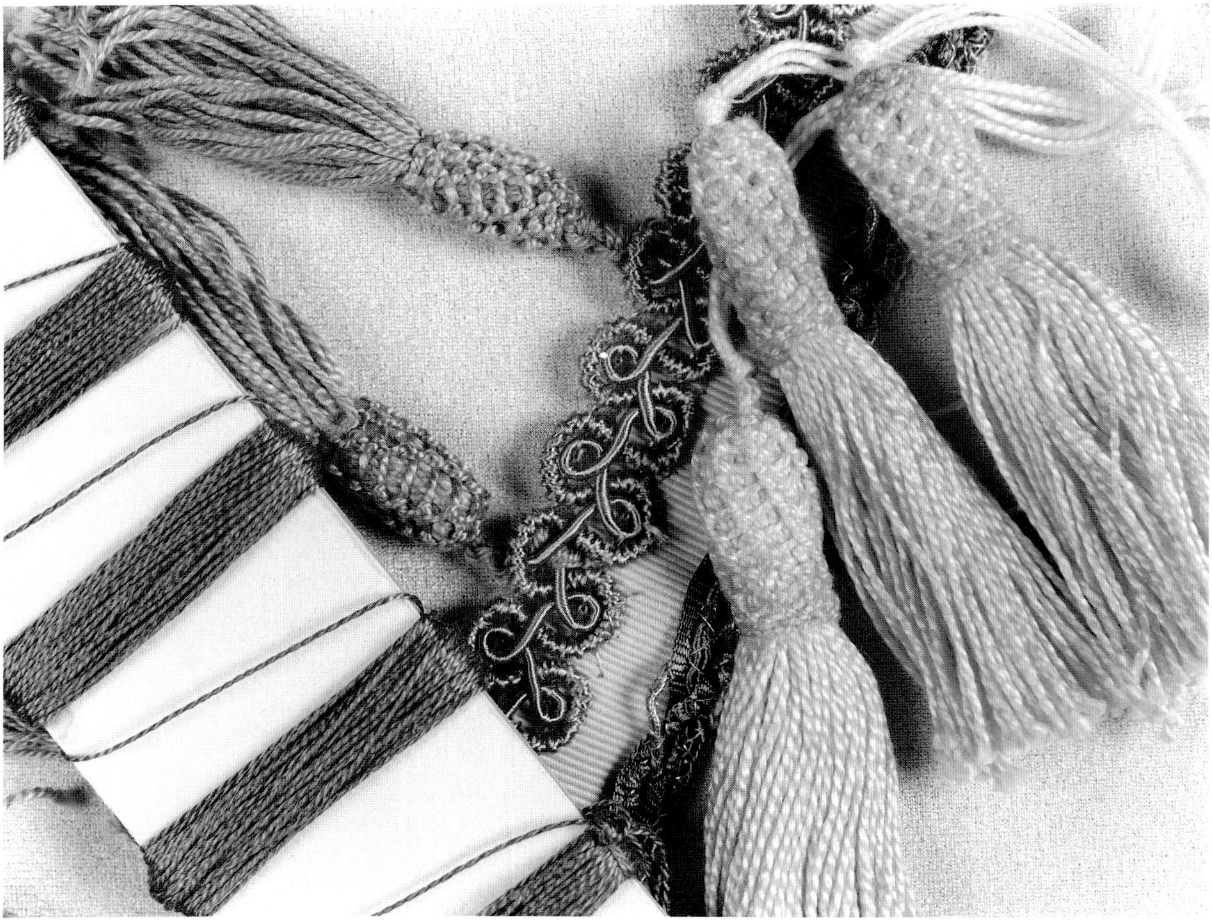

Detached buttonhole, braid, and mass production (also Plate II) – the braid is made by stitching together grosgrain ribbon, a purchased braid and a three strand plaited braid made from machine made cords.

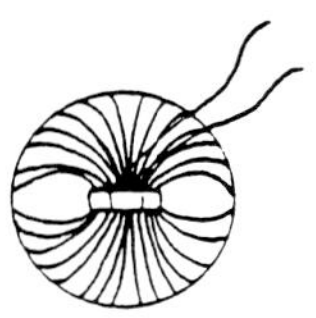

Fig. 2a

You are now ready to commence the detached buttonhole stitches:-

4. Looking down at the top of the tassel, as in Figure 2a, is the bar that ties the top of the tassel. Bring the needle out at the left side of the bar at A and work two detached buttonhole stitches around the bar at the left of the knot. Refer to Figure 2b. Then work two more detached buttonhole stitches on the bar on the right side of the knot.

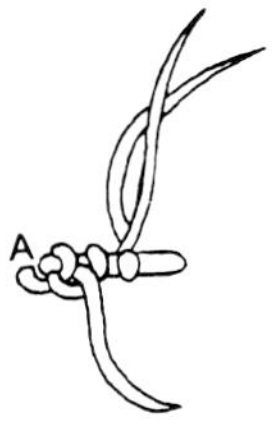

Fig. 2b

5. Turn the tassel around and make two more detached buttonhole stitches around the bar on the left-hand side of the knot and two further stitches on the bar to the right-hand side of the knot, from B to A.

This takes you back to the beginning and makes a foundation of eight loops. Refer Figure 2c.

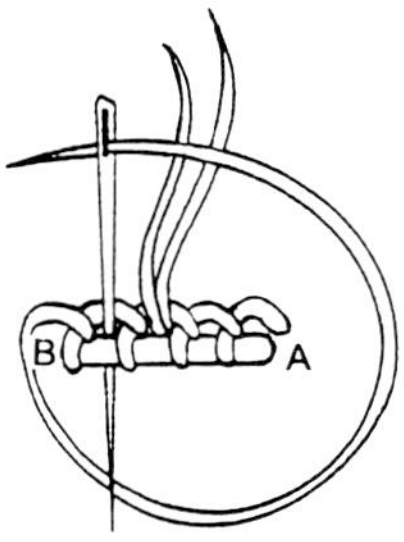

Fig. 2c

6. Continue taking detached buttonhole stitches in the previous row, going round and round in a spiral. Care needs to be taken with the tension of each stitch so that it is neither too tight nor too loose - practice will teach you the correct amount of tension. Very tight tension produces a narrow, thin tassel head whilst too little tension results in an open, loose mesh.

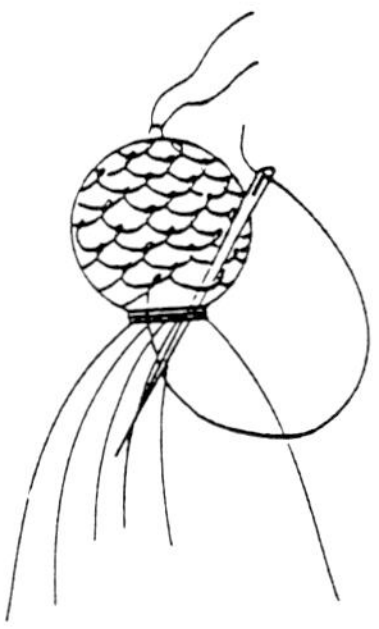

Fig. 2d

7. When you have detached buttonhole stitched to about three-quarters of the way down the tassel head, finish off the head by stitching through the head at the neck. That is, for every detached buttonhole stitch taken into the previous row, at the same time pass the needle under the neck thread pulling gently but firmly so that the mesh created by the detached buttonhole stitches spreads evenly to cover the head. Refer Figure 2d.

Running out of yarn

Should your yarn run out before you have finished detached buttonholing, leave the end of the yarn unfinished while you thread a new needle and yarn up through the skirt of the tassel bringing it out through the last worked loop. Continue detached buttonhole stitching for a couple of rows with the new yarn and then finish off the remaining short length into the skirt of the tassel.

Method 3 - Keyhole – Photo below

1. Make Basic Tassel No. 2.
2. Divide the tassel head in two. This is easily done as the cord ties the yarn in the middle. Thread the needle with a very long piece of yarn approximately 1 to 1.5 m (5 ft) up through the centre of the tassel skirt, coming out at the neck on the left hand side.
3. Detached buttonhole stitch up one side of the head around all the yarn being careful to count stitches as you go. When half way has been reached work around the holding yarn at the top which is the half way point of the tassel head. Care needs to be taken when assessing the half way point as the tying yarn tends to slip.
4. Detached buttonhole stitch the other half of the head with the same number of stitches as the first half.
5. Wind remaining yarn several times firmly around the neck, securing with several detached buttonhole stitches and trim the tails of this yarn the same length as the skirt.
6. The yarn which fastens the neck can also be covered with detached buttonhole to give an attractive finish, and decorated with stitches, beads or needleweaving. Refer to Chapters 3 and 6.

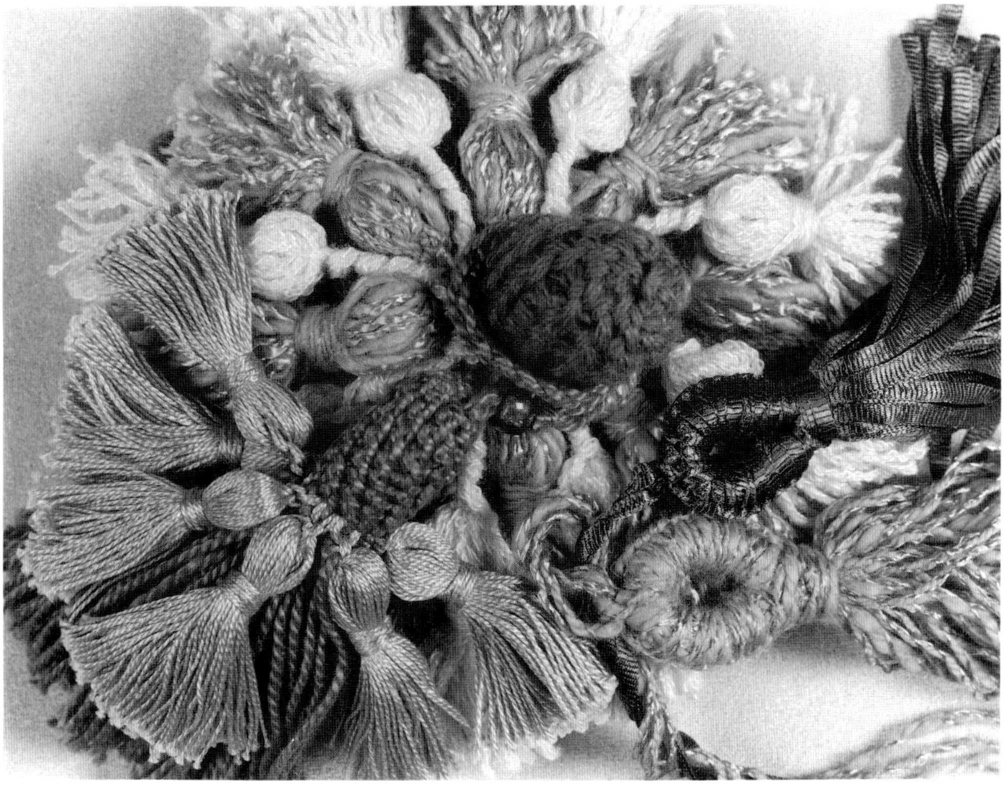

Left – multiple family tassels Right – keyhole tassels

Method 4 - Keyhole

The same method as No. 3 except that wrapping stitch is used as an alternative to buttonhole stitch.

Method 5 -Divided head – Photo below and page 26

Divide head into four or more portions and work detached buttonhole or wrap as described in methods 3 and 4 above.

Method 6 -Multiple heads – Photo page 26

Make more than one head by tying – two, three or more necks.

Method 7 -Multiple or 'family' tassels – Photos page 24 and page 26 and Figure 3

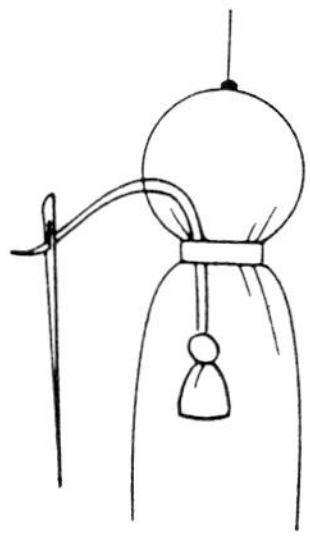

Fig. 3a

1. Make Basic Tassel No. 1 or 2.
2. Make eight more tassels either the same length or smaller than the length from the neck to the bottom of the skirt. Attach these eight tassels around the neck of the first as follows:-
3. Thread the holding cord through a tapestry needle and take it up and under the neck. Refer Figure 3a.

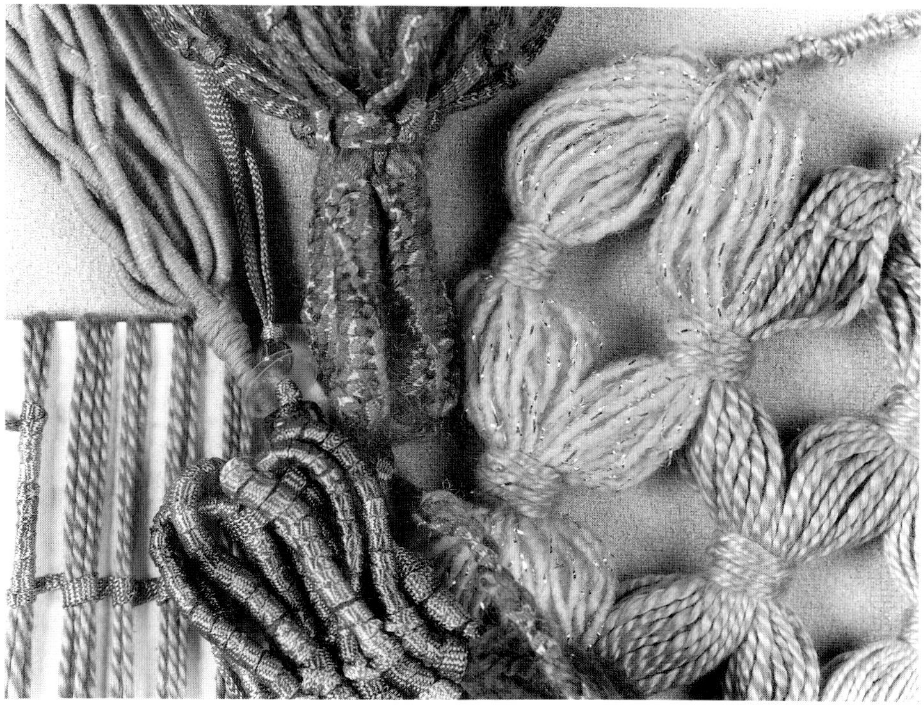

Top left – plaited machine wrapped cords with close satin stitch. Centre top – tassel head divided into four and detached buttonhole stitched. A fringe of yarn tied in overhand knots forms an overskirt. Bottom left – card template showing wrapping for a multiple divided head which is shown next to it. The tassel head was wrapped with a needle threaded with space dyed yarn – this is an alternative method to wrapping groups of cut yarn without a card template. Right – a number of tassels were divided in half and wrapped, creating a flat tassel. The holding cord is worked in twisted detached buttonhole.

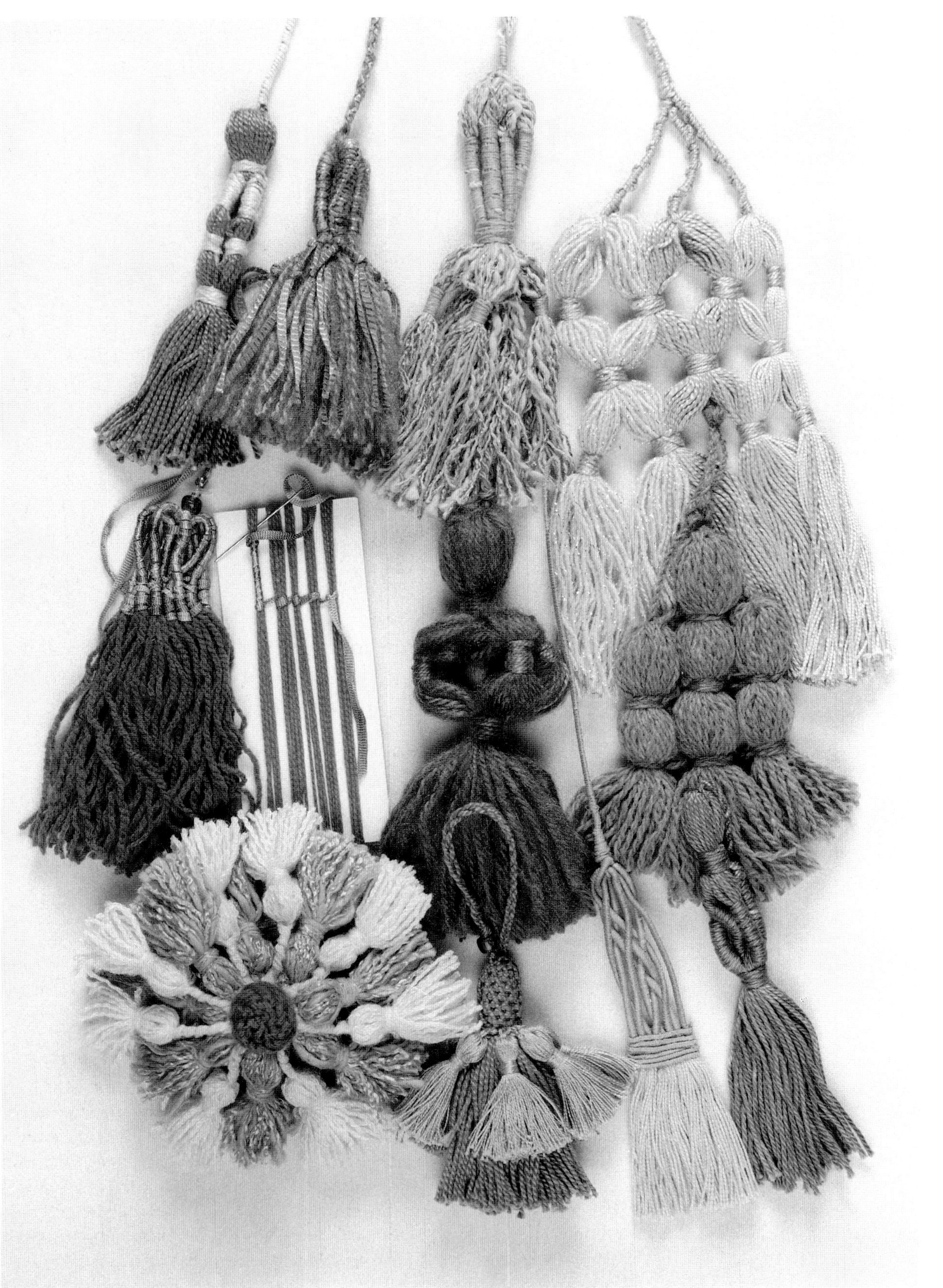

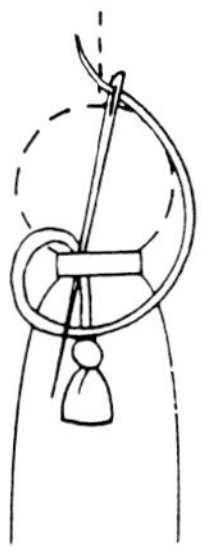
Fig. 3b

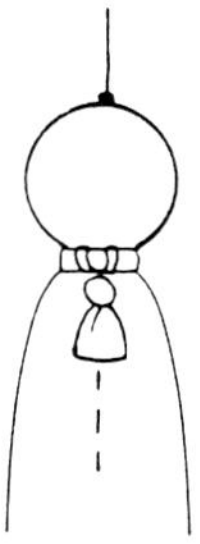
Fig. 3c

4. Make a loop, take the yarn from the top down behind the neck and over the loop. Pull firmly to secure. Refer Figure 3b.
5. Take the remaining yarn down through the small tassel, trimming it to the same length as the tassel skirt. Refer Figure 3c.

Method 8 - Beaded – Plate III

Plate III shows many different ways to make beaded tassels.

Thread waxed double lengths of machine sewing cotton or polyester covered cotton through a beading or No. 10 sharp needle. If available use a piece of beeswax sold at specialty embroidery and quilting shops, to draw the sewing thread through to strengthen it. Pick up the beads from a saucer or lid with the needle or by wetting the end of your finger where the beads will cling for easy pick up.

Looped beaded tassel

1. Make a knot at the end of the sewing cotton and pick up enough beads to form the desired length to double it and create a string of looped beads. Tie the end of the cotton with an overhand knot.
2. Repeat this process until you have enough loops of beads to create the desired thickness of the tassel skirt.
3. With a separate yarn wrap the tops of the bead loops together and take the wrapping thread up through a bead with a large hole so that the wrapped tops are concealed within the bead hole.
4. An alternative finish is to detached buttonhole the wrapped group of threads as for methods 1 or 2 (pages 16 and 22). You may first need to wrap some thicker yarn or quilt wadding at the top to pad the head before covering with detached buttonhole stitch.

Keyhole and multiple family. Top row Left - the neck is divided into three and wrapped at intervals. Second from left - the head is divided in four and worked in detached buttonhole stitch. An overskirt of space dyed knitting ribbon tied with overhand knots creates a fringed overskirt. Second from right - the head is divided in four and wrapped. The full skirt is divided to form a top layer of tassels wrapped at their necks. Right - three tassels are joined at the top with a twisted detached buttonhole cord. The heads are divided in two and wrapped as shown to create a flat tassel. This system may be used to make a fringe. Middle row Left - A tassel wrapped around a card as shown is joined at its neck by raised stem band stitch and wrapped with a needle threaded with space dyed knitting yarn. Middle - After the tassel is wound on the card template the first neck is tied in place. The rest is divided in three and wrapped as shown. A second neck is then wrapped and a wooden bead stitched in the middle to make the divided neck stand out. Right - multiple necks are tied on three tassels then they are stitched together side by side. Wooden beads are threaded through the centre of the multiple heads for padding. Bottom row Left and second from left - multiple family tassels. Second from right - Lengths of cut yarn are machine wrapped with close satin stitching and plaited together. A machine wrapped cord is tied around the neck and stitched in place. Right - the head is divided in four and wrapped part way between two necks.

Metal jewellery findings make attractive tassel heads and these tassels make attractive earrings.

Bead strings

Another method of making a beaded tassel is to attach bead strings individually to a strip of felt.

Felt or fabric head

A rectangle of felt or non-fraying fabric approximately 1 cm (.5 in) wide by 5 cm (2 in) long may be used. Attach the strings of beads onto the long side. The felt is then rolled up and stitched in place. Work detached buttonhole stitch over the felt or fabric. Embroidery stitches and more beads could also be worked onto the fabric head.

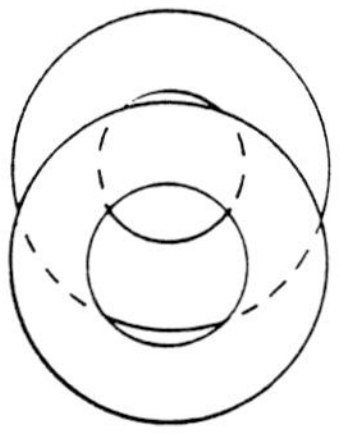

Fig. 4a

Method 9 - overhand knot – Plate IV

Cut a group of yarn lengths approximately 70 cm (27.5 in) long. Fold in two. Tie an overhand knot towards the folded end and attach a cord to the loop created by the folded end. Tassel ends may be trimmed straight, diagonally, at random or frayed.

Method 10 - flat knot – Plate IV

Using lengths of thread from the body of the tassel tie two or more detached buttonhole stitches to form the neck of the tassel.

Method 11 - pom pom – Plate IV and Figure 4

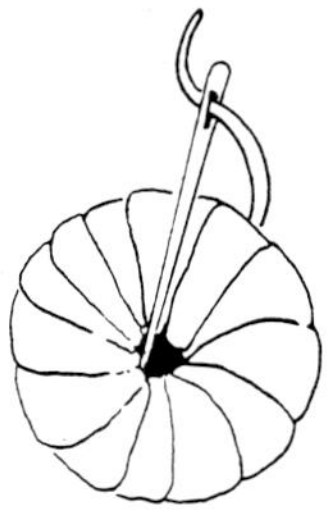

Fig. 4b

1. Cut out two circles of medium weight card with a large hole in the middle. The diameter of the circle depends on the required size of the finished pom pom. Figure 4a.
2. Wrap yarn around the two cards, through the hole, until the hole is packed and there is enough yarn to make a firm pom pom. Lengths of yarn may need to be rolled into balls small enough to fit through the hole, or a knitter's needle with a large eye could be threaded with long lengths of doubled yarn. Figure 4b.
3. When the card is thickly packed with yarn cut around the edge of the circle with a pair of sharp pointed scissors in the gap between the two pieces of card. Figure 4c.

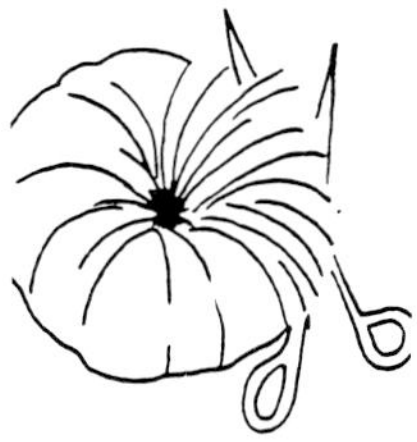

Fig. 4c

4. Tie a piece of yarn or holding cord around the middle of the cut threads in the gap between the two pieces of card with a firm reef knot. This tie becomes the attaching cord. Figure 4d.
5. Remove the cards and fluff the cut yarn to make a ball shape. Trim with a sharp pair of scissors if necessary.

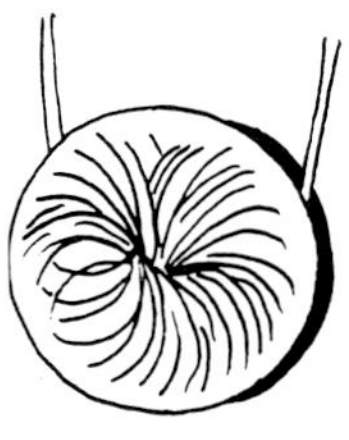

Fig. 4d

The size of the pom pom varies depending on the size of the card template and the size of the hole. Pom poms can be used as bobbles sewn to braid to create a fringe and to decorate a large tassel as seen on Plate XI. They are also attractive used to finish off cords and decorate clothing.

Method 12 - leather – Plate IV

Leather has a character of its own and its main benefit is that it doesn't fray. If possible sew it together otherwise use craft glue.

Method 13 - ribbon – Plate IV

Any type of ribbon can be used to produce distinctive unique tassels. Machine or hand embroidered ribbon is attractive when used in lengths and combined with tassels made from other yarns.

Method 14 - felt – Plate IV

Felt is versatile as it doesn't fray and combined with machine stitching produces quick results. It should be laundered with care.

Method 15 - feathers – Plate IV

Many colourful feathers are available to tie together or combine with beads and cords.

Method 16 - horizontal and vertical wrapping – Plates IV, V and VI

Horizontal wrapping is described in the instructions for wrap knot, as well as in the instructions for needleweaving.

Vertical wrapping is made over horizontally wrapped yarn. Use the horizontal wrapping as a core and padding.

Method 17 - knotted ball – Plate XVI and Photo page 30

Small double knots

1. Tie overhand knots about 24 mm (1 in) apart on any kind of yarn.
2. Cut the yarn after every two knots to make short lengths.
3. Load a sharp needle with any matching or contrasting yarn with a knot on the end. Take the needle through the centre of the yarn between the two knots and thread ten or more short knotted lengths. This string of 'knots' then becomes a tassel.

This tassel may be used for fringing or tied with others in bunches.

Large double knots

1. Tie six overhand knots on top of each other. A large tapestry needle will assist in guiding the placement of each overhand knot.

   Follow steps 2 and 3 above as for small double knots.

Method 18 - plaited – Plate XVI and Photo page 30

Make approximately ten or more monkey's fist knots, or cylindrical Turk's head knots containing wooden beads and tie together in a bunch to make a tassel or attach to a braid to make a fringe.

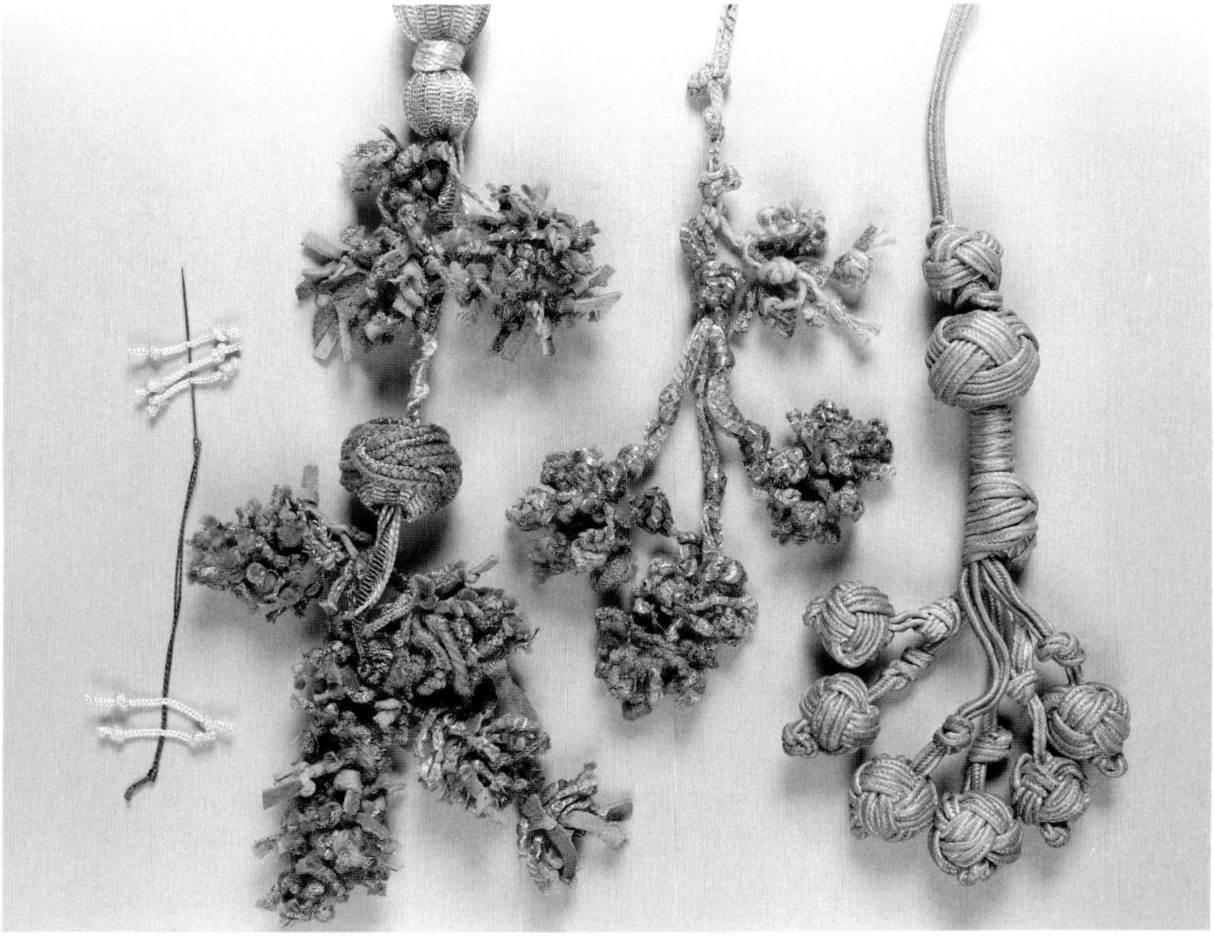

Knotted ball and plaited. Left - the needle on the left threaded with yarn shows the method of joining the knotted yarn or cord to make the knotted ball, small double knots, tassel shown to the right of the needle. The three wooden beads incorporated in the tassel have been wrapped with space dyed knitting ribbon and the large lower bead has been covered with a cylindrical Turk's head knot which was first made on a dowel stick then slipped over the wrapped bead. Centre - knotted ball tassel, large double knots, which are assembled in the same method shown on the left, with needle and yarn. Right - plaited tassel - cylindrical Turk's head knots are slipped onto wooden beads and tied together.

Method 19 - crocheted swirl

Plate XII and Photo page 32 show examples of crocheted swirl tassels which are made as follows;-

1 Crochet a chain of ten to twenty loops.

2 Work five to ten trebles in each chain to the end, twisting each frill neatly as you work.

3 Fasten off.

Yarn, hook and length of chain may be varied.

Chapter 2

Decorative and Special Effects

General Variations

Chapter 2 shows many ways to vary, decorate and embellish basic tassels. Experiments in creating your own individual tassels are fun experiences and random combinations of some of the techniques shown in this book allow the creator innumerable variations to produce a unique tassel.

Cord

- vary the nature of the cord by changing the materials, width and length
- add beads and stitchery
- make a feature of the cord

Head

- add extra heads by making matching or contrasting covered foundations
- incorporate found objects - seed pods, shells, sticks
- embellish with beads and stitchery
- make a feature of the head

Neck

- change the distance of the neck from the cord to the bottom of the skirt to change the proportion of the whole tassel
- make more than one neck
- make a feature of the neck

Skirt

- leave the skirt looped
- attach beads
- cut skirt unevenly or in multiple layers
- create more than one skirt per tassel head
- make a feature of the skirt

Whole tassels

- combine several similar tassels in groups or bunches
- combine two or more different tassels in one group or bunch
- make a unique feature tassel

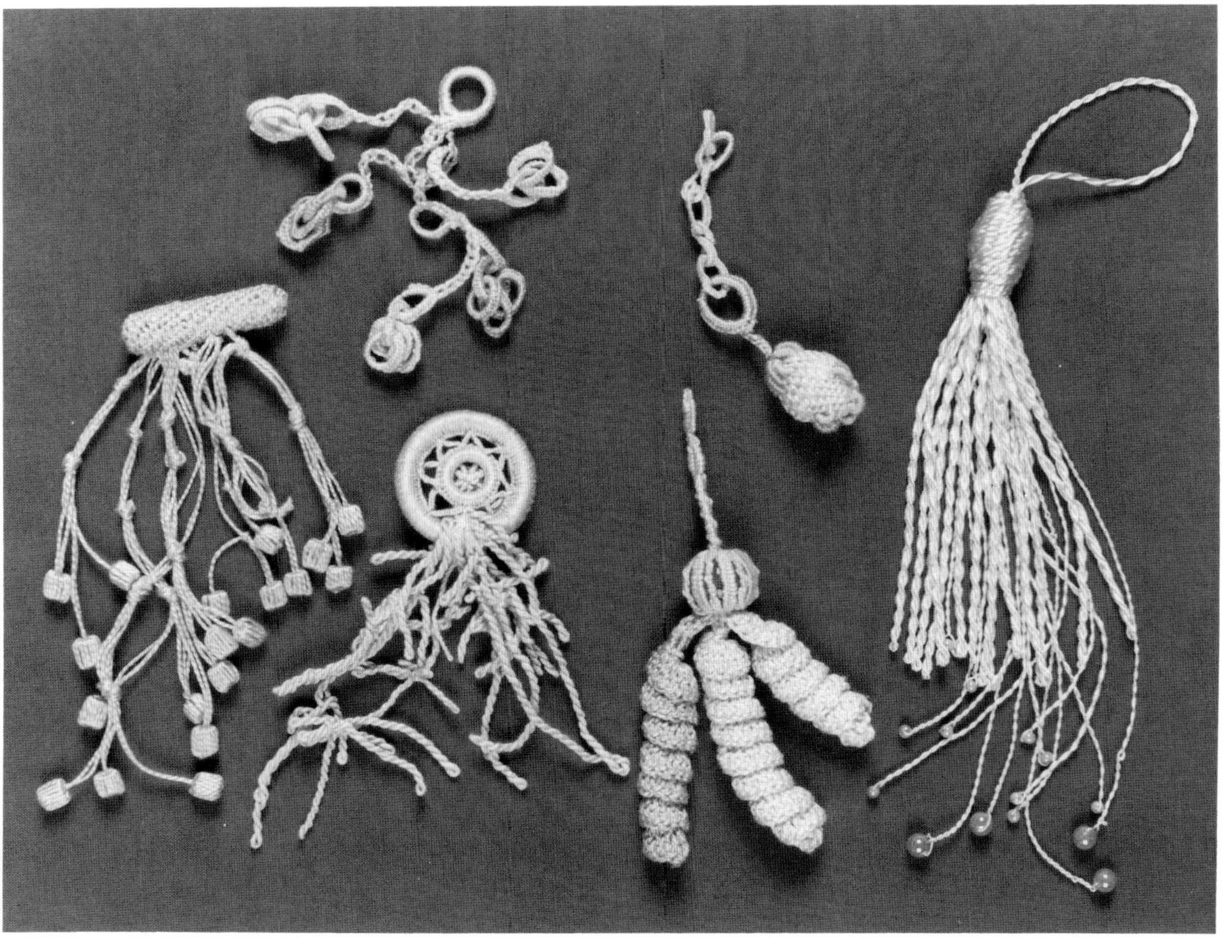

Crocheted swirls. Top row Left - Tassel made of soft needlewoven rings worked over a pencil. To achieve the chain effect place a finished ring next to the pencil and thread the core yarn through the ring and around the pencil, then detached buttonhole the core yarn. Right - A chained cord holds a ball of quilt wadding which has been covered with detached buttonhole stitch then embroidered with bullion knot stitch. Bottom row Left - A wooden dowel plug is first covered with fabric then embroidered with detached buttonhole stitch. Wrapped 'beads' of small lengths of plastic tubing are wrapped with coton perle No. 5 and the holding cords tied with overhand knots. Second from left - The head consists of two detached buttonholed plastic rings joined with needleweaving and a back stitch woven web worked in the centre. Randomly twisted cords made on the sewing machine are stitched to the ring. Second from right - Crocheted swirls, made by Eileen Gale, hang from a bead covered with woven plain weave needleweaving hanging from a twisted detached buttonhole cord. Right - Twisted machine made cords, some with beads attached to the bottom hang from a head stitched with a twisted cord.

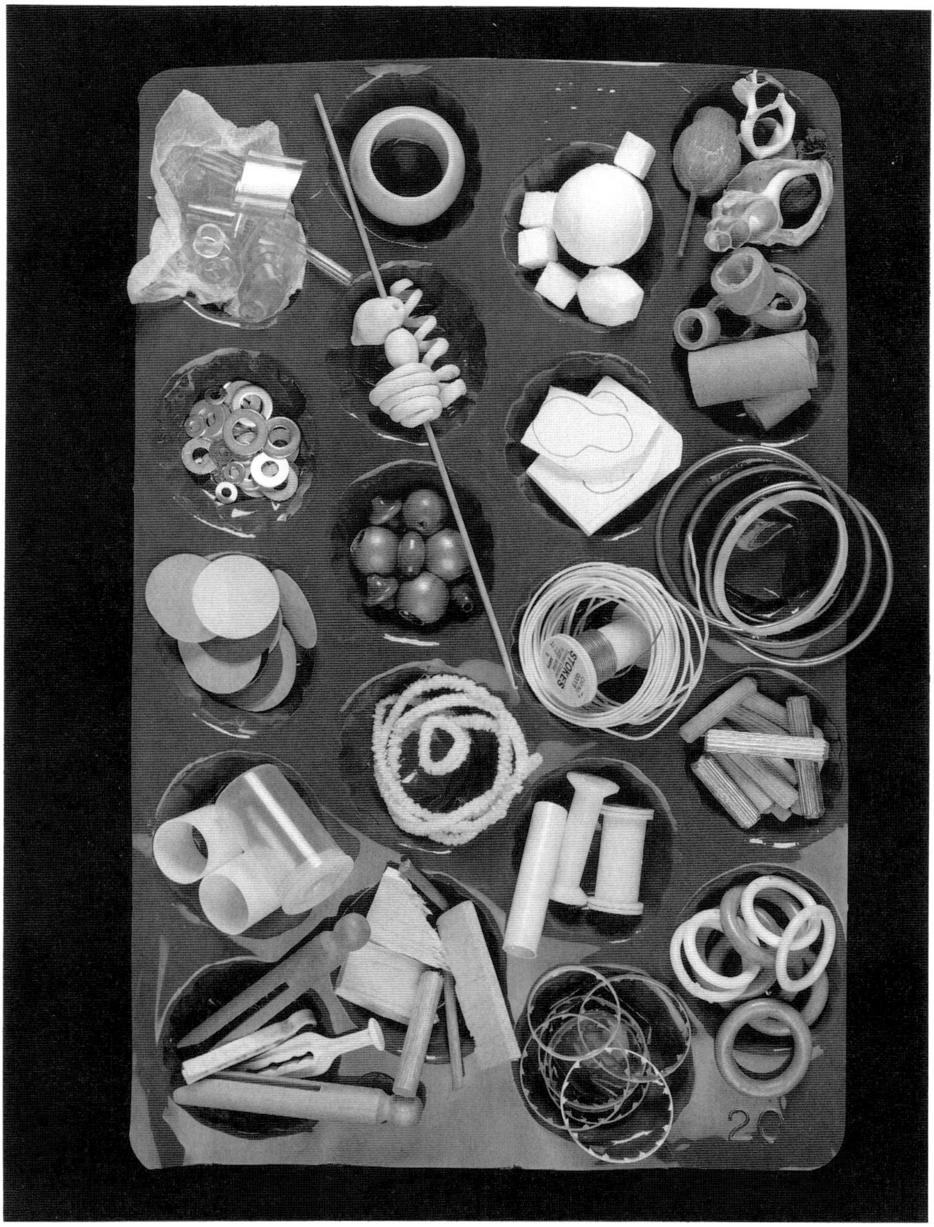

Mango box. Left hand row, top to bottom - cut lengths of plastic tubing; metal washers; discs of card and plastic; plastic cylinders from pill bottles and film containers; various pegs including 'dolly' pegs from craft shop. Second row from left, top to bottom - serviette ring; shapes and beads made from modelling clay strung onto a wooden skewer stick; wooden beads; pipe cleaners; balsa wood and wooden dowel sticks. Second row from right, top to bottom - polystyrene ball and pieces of polystyrene; fomecore; fuse wire and florist's wire; empty cotton reels; soft plastic rings from plastic bottles. Right hand row - top to bottom - shells and gum nuts; wooden cylinders; plastic bangles and metal rings; wooden dowel plugs; plastic and wooden rings.

Foundations and padding materials

Many everyday materials can be adapted to make tassel moulds. Beads with large holes, modelling clay, plastic objects, plastic tubing cut into shorter lengths, paper strips and glue, polystyrene shapes, cardboard cylinders, empty sewing cotton reels and spools, cotton balls rolled with PVA glue, felt and cotton wadding sewn into shapes - even serviette rings, curtain rings, plastic milk bottle ring tops, wooden clothes pegs, small pieces of cut foam sponge enclosed in a fabric bag. In other words almost anything may be considered for recycling as tassel moulds.

Photo page 33 is a recycled fruit box which provides practical storage for foundations and shows many different and useful materials.

Photo page 35 shows different materials before and after covering.

Using a mould

A mould is a frame which gives shape and body for distinctive tasselmaking. Moulds used by manufacturers are often made of wood with a hole down the centre through which yarn and cords may be threaded and yarn ends buried. A mould which historically comes in many shapes and sizes could be described as a very large wooden bead and these specially shaped wooden moulds are generally made for industry and are not usually purchased from retail stores. However, alternative moulds could be large beads, moulded clay or other materials as suggested above and as shown in photos page 33 and page 35.

There are numerous ways to make a tassel using a mould, depending on the design and the availability of materials and some examples are described below:-

Simple tassel moulds – Photo page 36

A simple example of using a mould is to buy plastic ends for curtain rods or use plastic bottle tops.

1. Make a hole in the top. A hole has been cut in the top of the curtain rod ends. A hole has been hammered into the top of the plastic bottle top with a large, thick, sharp nail.

2. Glue a long twisted or purchased cord around the mould in a spiral. Work from the top down. Don't put all the glue on at once all over the mould but apply row by row as you spiral down, ensuring that a little glue is also applied to the previous row of cording.

3. Roll approximately 20 cm (8 in) of made or purchased fringe and attach it to a holding cord.

4. Thread the cord and skirt into the mould and bring the cord out through the hole.

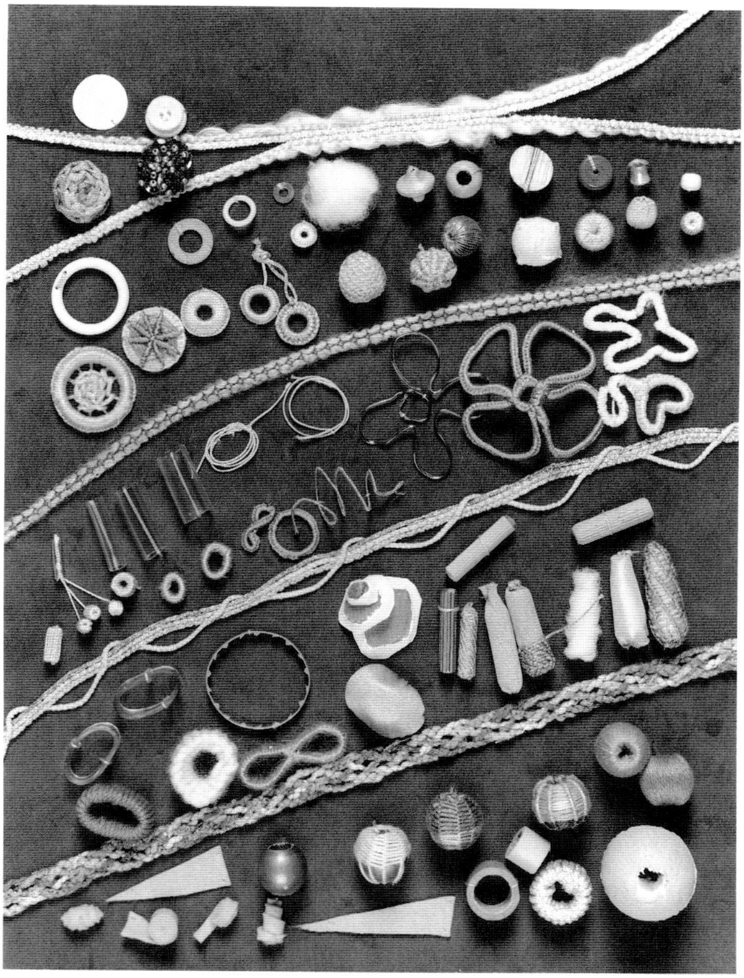

Before and after – Four different machine made cords divide up this page from top down: 1. A thick cord and a bubbly cotton knitting yarn were joined together with a machine 'feather' stitch using metallic thread to make the double braid. Two lengths of double braids are shown joined together at their thickest point. 2. Two machine made cords are joined together with a decorative diamond machine made stitch. 3. Three machine made cords are joined together then a fourth is looped over the first and stitched on by machine. 4. Machine made cords are woven to make a five strand braid.

The items on this page show the 'before' and 'after' of covering various foundation materials: Top left - A circle of card is shown first. It is then shown covered with chain stitched fabric gather stitched over the card. To the right of this a purchased plastic button covering kit is shown and below it the finished button is shown covered with beading on fabric.

First row - left to right - Underneath a plastic curtain ring two ways of covering are illustrated using detached buttonhole stitch and woven webs; two different sizes of metal washer and small plastic rings are shown covered with detached buttonhole stitch; a ball of cotton quilt wadding is stitched into a ball shape and then covered with detached buttonhole stitch; a wooden bead is covered with back stitch web stitch; another wooden bead is shown wrapped with yarn; half a wooden bead is shown covered with stretch fabric; the last three are a wooden bead, a glass jug bead and a plastic jug bead covered in detached buttonhole stitch or wrapping.

Second row - The first four items are various sizes of plastic tubing cut into short lengths and wrapped or detached buttonhole stitched. Next to this a loop of yarn is detached buttonhole stitched to make a soft ring. These soft rings may be worked around a pencil, a dowel, or even your fingers. The rest of the row shows different types of wire covered with machine zig-zag stitch or detached buttonhole stitch.

Third row - The first three rings are plastic shown covered with wrapping and detached buttonhole stitch. The soft bottle top ring is easily manipulated, after stitching, into interesting shapes. Next to this is shown fomecore board sculpted with a Stanley knife into shapes which have been glued together and covered with fabric. The rest of the row shows different ways to cover dowel plugs. They may be covered with detached buttonhole stitch, fabric or both or firstly padded into shapes with quilt wadding and then covered with fabric and detached buttonhole stitch.

Bottom row - Triangles of felt are rolled into 'beads'. This method is very effective used with leather as shown in Plate VIII: wooden beads are shown firstly wrapped with yarn then worked over the top with raised stem band or back stitch; wooden cylindrical shapes were first painted then detached buttonholed or wrapped with yarn; a polystyrene ball is shown painted and pierced with a hole ready for making up.

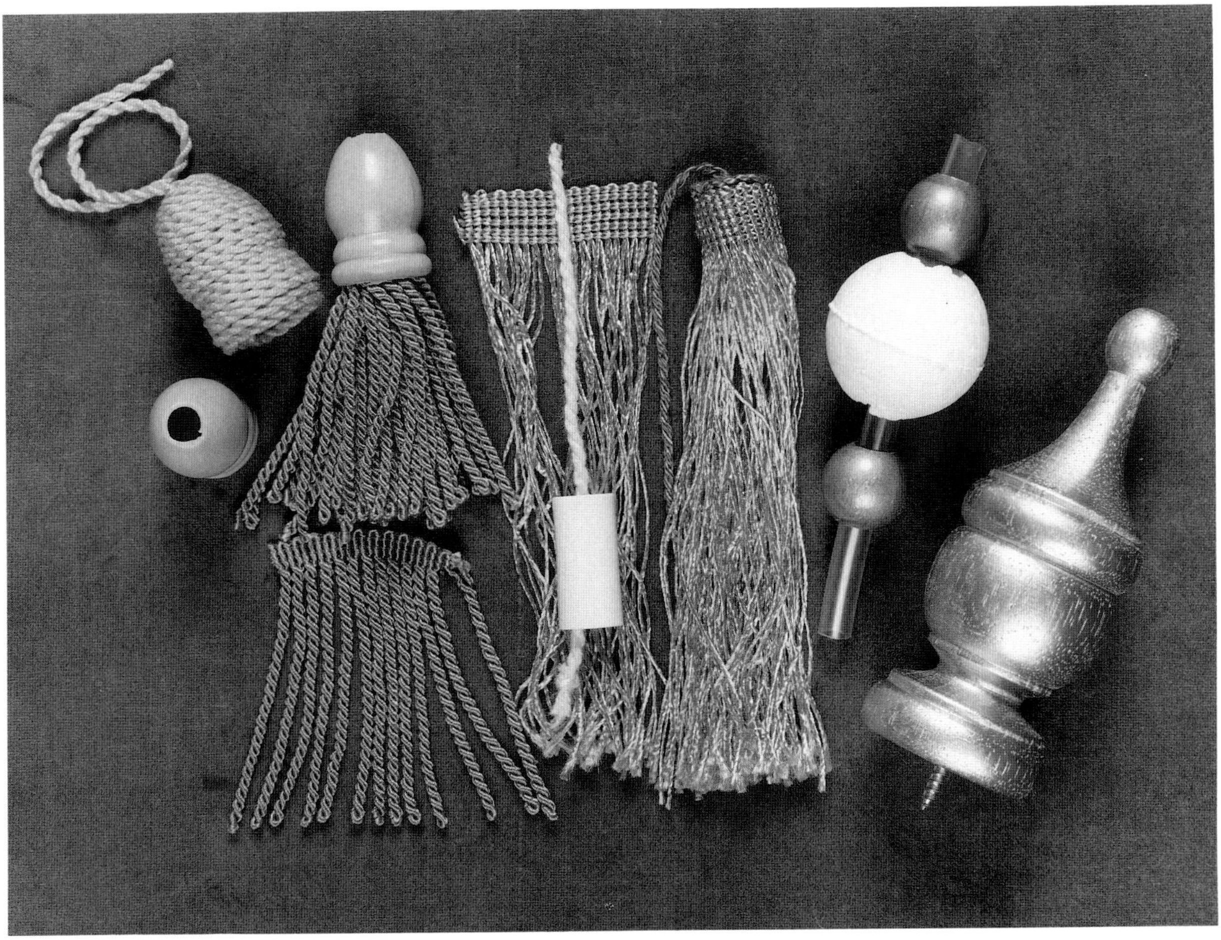

Using a mould (curtain rod ends). Left - a hole has been cut in the top of a plastic curtain rod end and a twisted cord glued onto it. Second from left - a purchased fringe is rolled and glued into the curtain rod end. Third from left - a hole has been nailed into the top of a plastic bottle top and a holding cord threaded through and knotted at the bottom to hold it in place. Third from right - shows a purchased fringe glued around the plastic bottle top. The top of the lid is concealed by a metal washer detached buttonhole stitched in a matching coloured yarn. Second from right - possible foundations and moulds for making a tassel are wooden beads and a polystyrene ball threaded onto plastic tubing. The plastic tubing allows the holding cord to be threaded through to it so it can be secured to the base of the tassel to keep the units together. Right - a wooden curtain rod end has been spray painted with metallic gold. It is shown in Plate XVI made up into a decorative tassel.

If you can't make a hole in the mould leave a length of holding cord at the top and follow step 2 page 34. Then glue the rolled skirt into the mould.

The above photo also shows a possible mould arrangement of a polystyrene ball with two beads threaded onto plastic tubing.

This photo also shows a large wooden curtain rod end which is incorporated in a tassel in Plate XVI. Glue and stitch a strip of soft fabric or old stocking firmly onto the screw to facilitate the attachment of a tassel skirt.

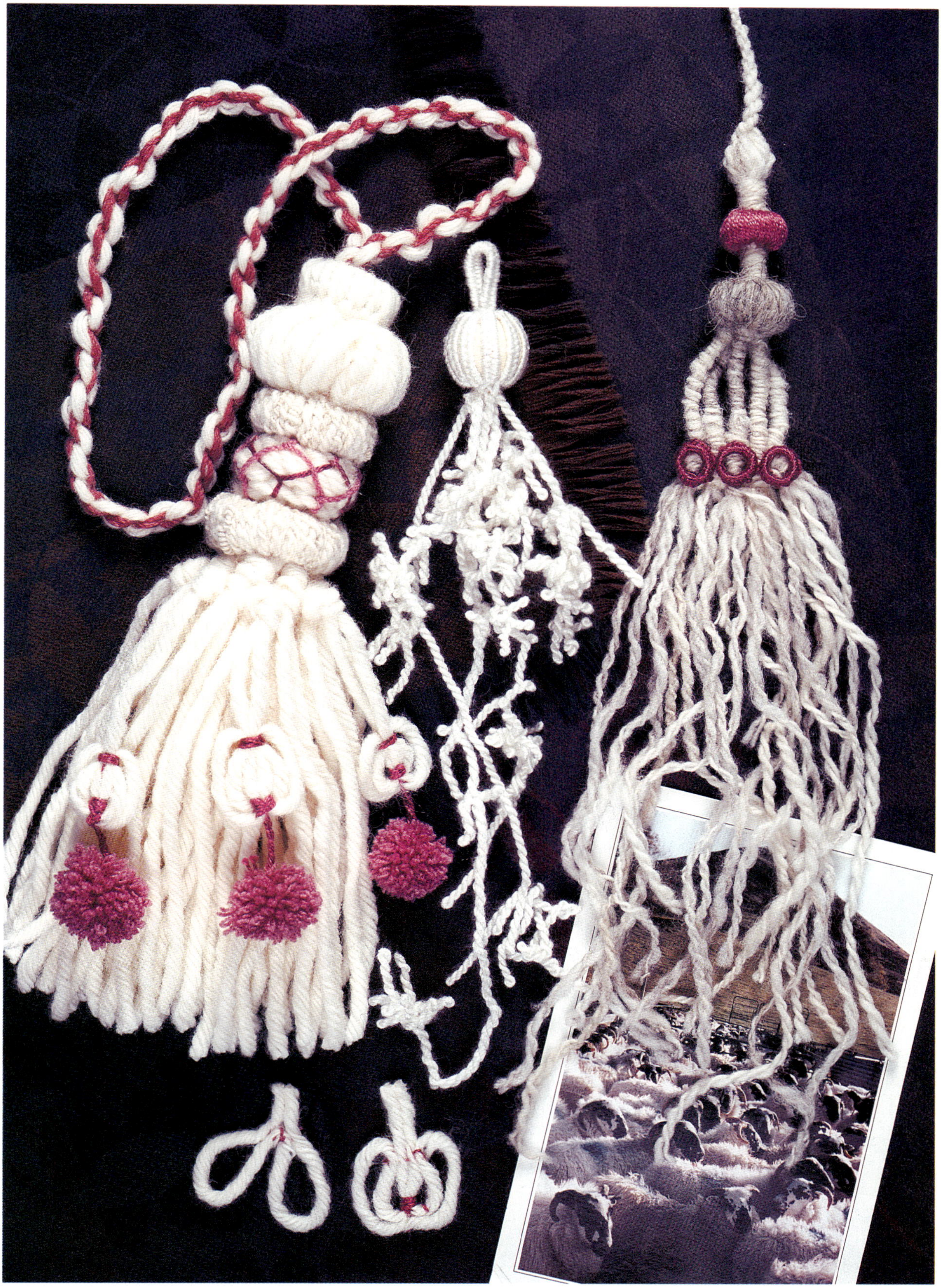

Plate V

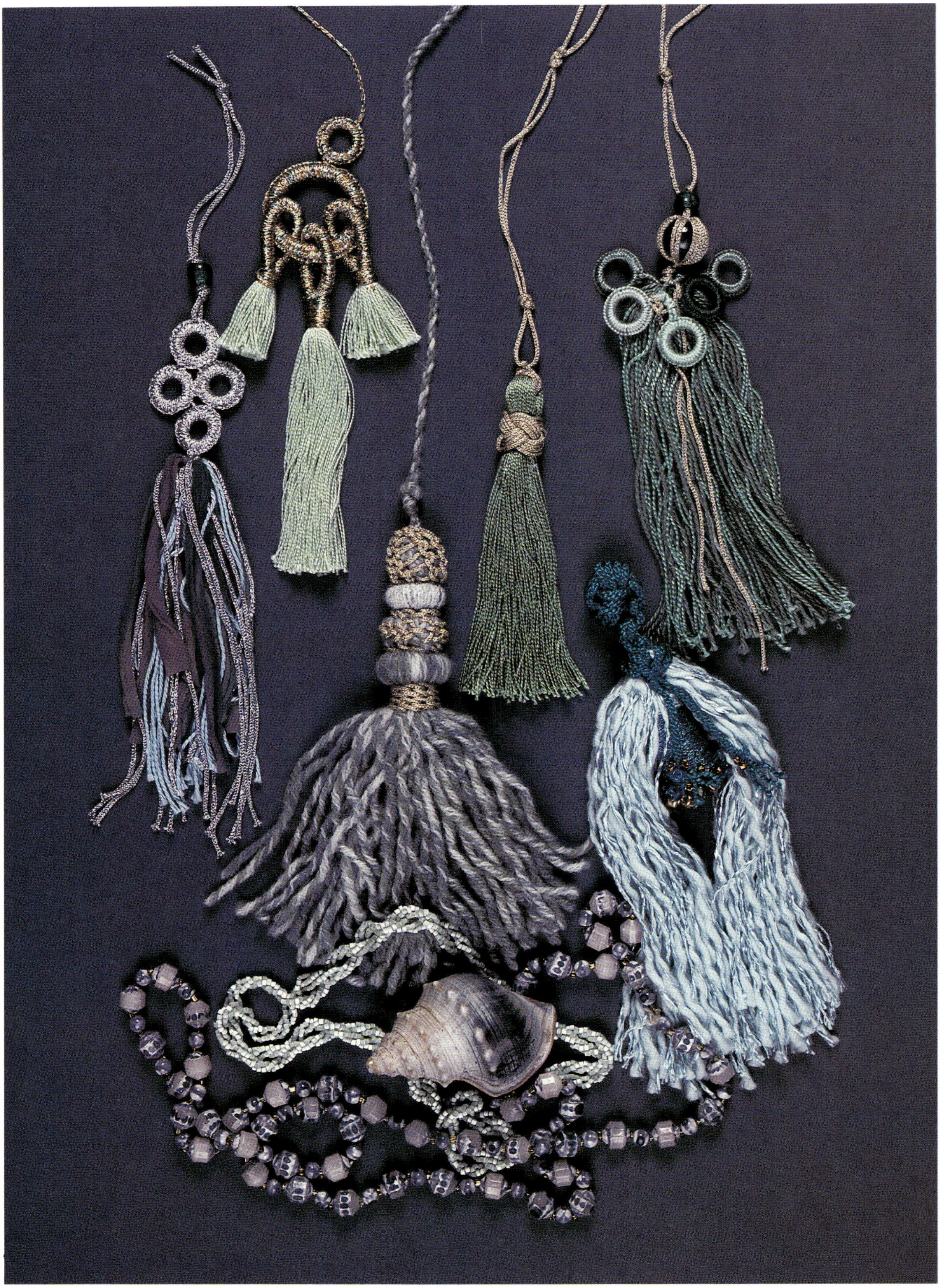

Plate VI

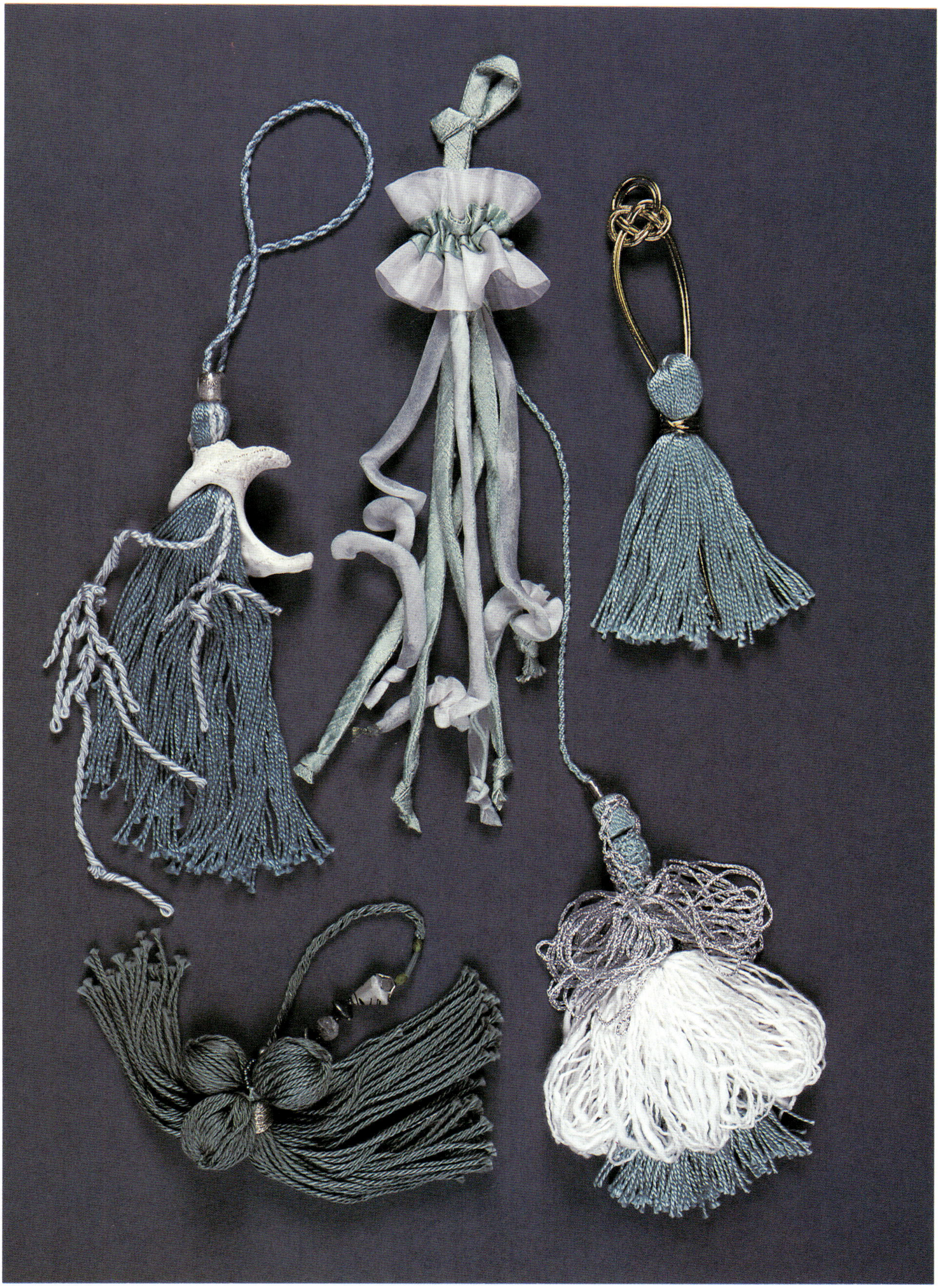

Plate VII

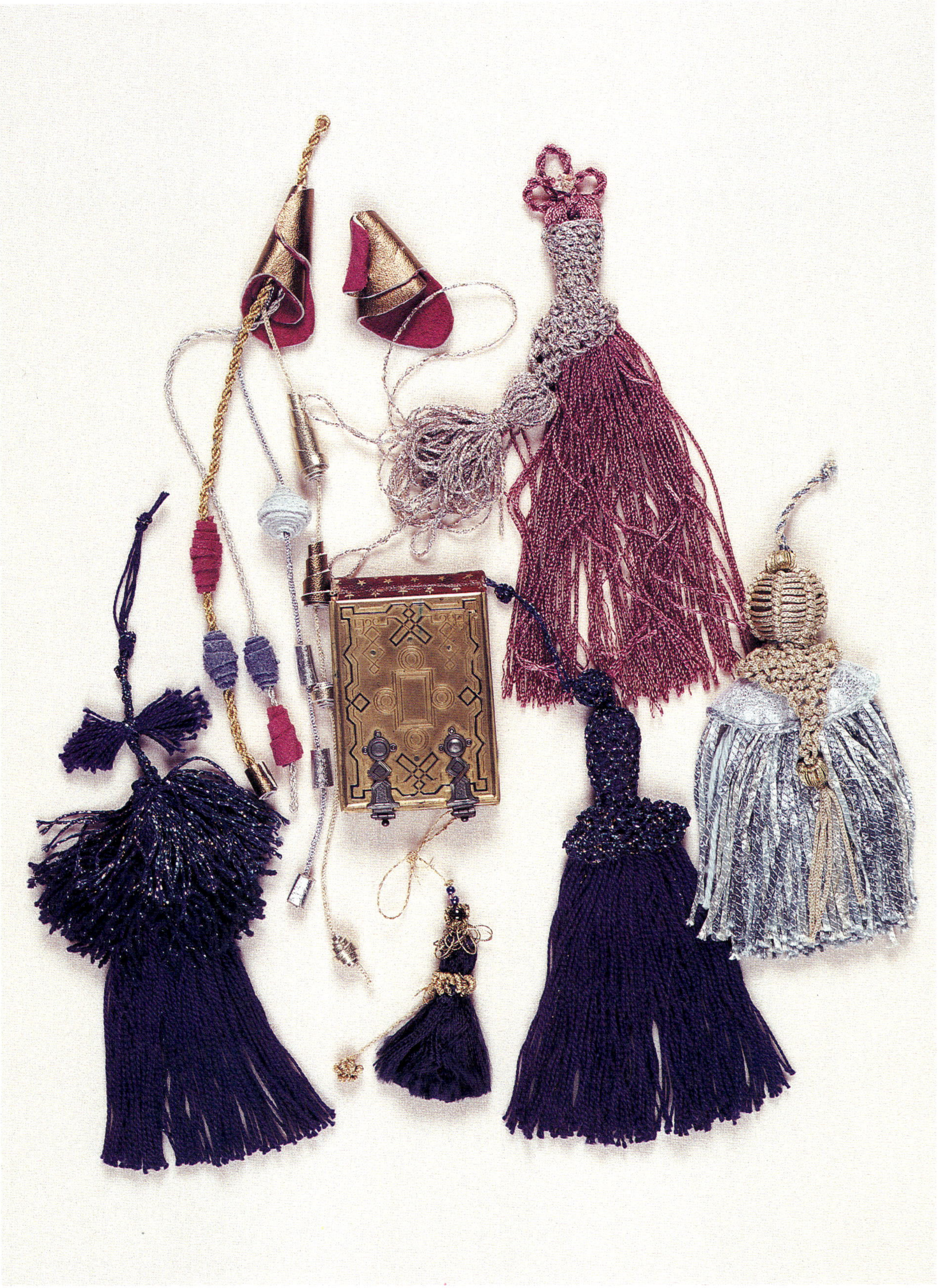

Plate VIII

Plate V Wool

Wool makes up into lovely tassels which can be chunky or fine. Left – Top of tassel down – Twisted cord with two colours, detached buttonhole plastic tubing; head; three necks vertically wrapped while the centre neck has been embellished with two rows of Cretan stitch, one row on top of the other; the skirt is decorated with overhand knots at the top and pom poms attached to loop knots. The two knots under the tassel show the steps required to make the loop knot. Centre – Top of tassel down – A loop of woven, plain weave needle weaving holds the head which is a wooden bead covered in the same stitch as the loop. The skirt is twisted cording allowed to twist at random, Right – The tassel has two horizontally wrapped necks and two round bead like shapes which are actually vertically wrapped yarns. Three soft detached buttonhole rings decorate the top of a wispy handspun wool skirt. The soft detached buttonhole rings were worked around a pencil.

Plate VI Sea and Shore

Top row – left to right. Left - Four small plastic rings covered with detached buttonhole stitch are joined together to form the head while the skirt is made of yarn, cording and 6 mm (.5 in) strips of dyed pantyhose. Second left - The three tassels attached to a detached buttonhole curtain ring were made of lengths of cut coton perle No. 5 yarn which were first wrapped in the middle, threaded onto the ring then the neck wrapped last. Second from right - A simple but elegant tassel is made of coton perle No. 5 with a cylindrical Turk's head knot slipped in place at the neck. Right - A wrapped wooden bead holds a skirt in 4 ply crochet yarn. The neck is festooned with small detached buttonholed plastic rings. Bottom row - left to right. Left - Wool yarn tassel with a twisted cord, detached buttonhole head followed by vertical wrapping, horizontal raised chain band stitch, vertical wrapping, horizontal raised stem band neck above a full skirt. Right - The head is a monkey's fist knot holding a skirt of bubbly knitting yarn. The decorative foundation is made from a strip of felt rolled into a cylindrical shape, then wrapped with metallic yarn and stitched with beads.

Plate VII Rouleaux

Top row - left to right. Left – Basic Tassel No. 2 held by a twisted cord and a jug bead is made of No.5 coton perle. It has been pulled through the hole of a shell skeleton and a randomly twisted cord over the skirt gives an impression of seaweed. Centre – A cylinder of ribbon has been gathered to form the neck of this tassel which is made of knotted rouleaux cords which have been threaded with coloured yarn, pulled into gathers and tied at the end with an overhand knot. Right – A Basic Tassel No. 1 made of coton perle No. 5 is held by a Josephine knot - looped, made of gold cord. Bottom row - left to right.Left – A beaded twisted cord holds a triple headed tassel made of 4 ply crochet yarn. A wrapped wooden bead forms the foundation of each head. Right - Two looped overskirts are attached to a tassel with a detached buttonhole head. Chain stitch is embroidered over the head and the wrapped plastic tubing on top of it.

Plate VIII Arabic Book

Top row Left - The head is made from a shaped leather and suede overskirt. Cording and twisted cords form the skirt. Triangular and rectangular leather strips have been rolled around the cords and attached with glue to form 'beads'. Middle - Shaped leather and suede overskirt rolled in an alternative way. Right - A Basic Tassel No. 2 was first made of rayon yarn. Detached buttonhole was then worked three quarters of the way from the neck up the head. A detached buttonhole skirt, shaped down to one side is worked from the neck downwards. A looped Basic Tassel No. 1 is attached to the skirt. The holding cord was twisted, made into three loops and decorated with beads. Bottom row Left - Two overskirts of metallic knitting yarn are tied over a Basic Tassel No. 2 made from coton-perle No. 5. A bunch of yarn is stitched into the holding cord which is worked in twisted detached buttonhole needleweaving. Second from left - A small notebook with a metal Arabic cover more than seventy years old holds a small Basic Tassel No. 1 made of soft ribbon. The neck is embroidered with bullion knot stitch in gold yarn with beads and gold yarn loops decorate the head and a bead covered in gold bullion knots hangs from the neck. Third from left - A Basic Tassel No. 2 made from coton perle No. 5 is decorated with detached buttonhole stitch from the cord to the neck and stitches are increased from the neck down to form a peplum overskirt. Right - A wooden bead is worked in back stitch web to form the head. The neck has a shaped fabric overskirt on top of which is worked another skirt of detached buttonhole stitch which is finished off with its own beaded tassel. The skirt contains a basic tassel plus an overskirt of knitting ribbon. The overskirt tied to the neck of the basic tassel gives a fullness to the skirt without giving the tassel a large head thus enabling it to be pulled up into the hole of the bead covered in back stitched web.

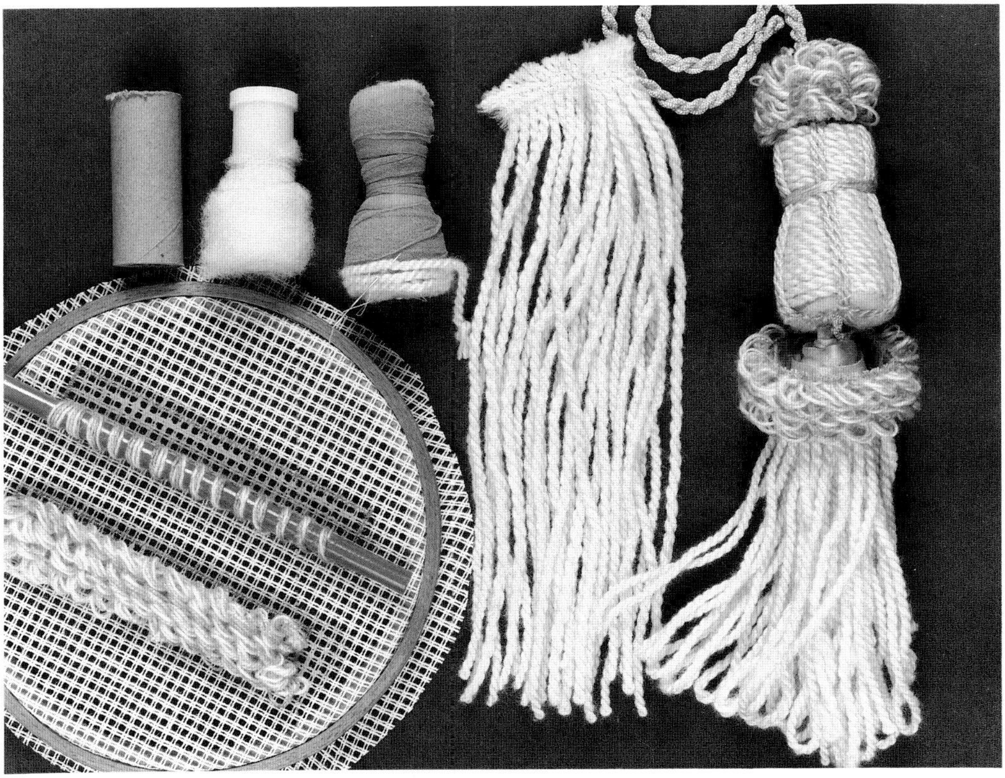

Making a dressed mould. Top left - a plastic cotton reel or wooden cylinder may be covered with wadding which can be trimmed into shape with sharp scissors. It is then covered with a strip of cut stocking. A twisted cord is stitched to the shape which is then vertically wrapped with twisted cord and tied. Bottom left - Collars of Ghiordes knot stitch are first worked on canvas. Second from right - a fringe of twisted cords is shown in the process of being prepared. Right - The tassel is shown ready for assembly.

Making a dressed mould

1. Cut out a strip of quilt wadding and wrap it around one half of a cotton reel, making a narrower central area. Stitch into place.
2. Repeat 1 above on the other half of the reel.
3. Trim with sharp scissors to the desired shape.
4. Cut 12 mm (.5 in) strips of old stocking or pantyhose and wrap around the wadding, tightening and padding further to form the desired shape.

5. Make or buy a cord approximately 3 m (3.4 yds) or more depending on the size of the mould and stitch it horizontally around the shape.
6. Using another cord approximately 2.5 metres (2.75 yds) or more depending on the size of the mould, in the same or contrasting colour, wrap it vertically through the hole and stitch it in place. Photo page 42 shows five vertical double wraps of cord. Stitch into place as you wrap.
7. Wrap the narrowest part of the mould with yarn to secure the vertical wraps.

The dressed mould is now ready to be decorated and combined with other elements to make the tassel.

Photo page 42 shows canvas in a hoop which has been worked with Ghiordes knot. Refer page 86 for instructions.

Photo page 42 also shows an example of the order of assembling the tassel. From top to bottom:- 1. cord, 2. ring of Ghiordes knot loops. 3. covered mould, 4. another ring of Ghiordes knot loops, 5. skirt.

Fomecore or featherweight mounting board

A very useful material for sculpturing shapes is fomecore or featherweight mounting board available from framers and art suppliers. This product comprises a sandwich of two pieces of medium weight card glued to a thin layer of polystyrene foam. It is easy to cut with a very sharp craft or Stanley knife. Refer to photo page 35 and Figure 5 for details of this procedure.

Method

1. Draw a shape in pencil on the cardboard and score the shape gently through the first layer of card. Refer to Figure 5.
2. Cut through the fomecore firmly with several strokes. If cutting a straight line use a metal ruler. Curved lines require more care, the secret being to score carefully and correctly for the first cut. When you've cut through most of the card you can turn the card over to finish the process by cutting from the back towards the front. Please remember to cut carefully and not with heavy, long flourishes towards you as the blade is very sharp. Do not attempt to use sharp cutting knives when tired or cross.

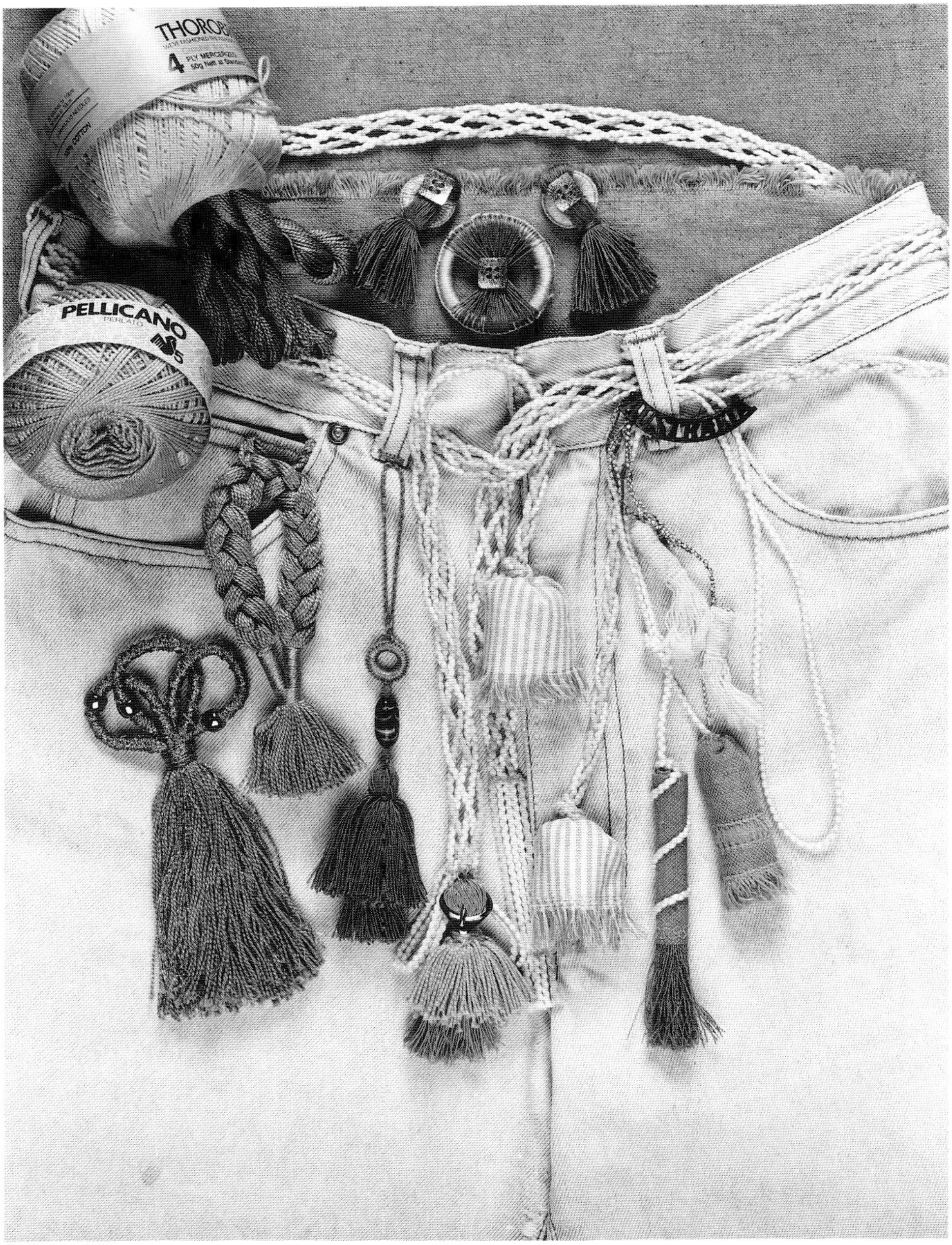

Decorative tassel heads. Top row - trimmings are made from detached buttonhole washers and a plastic curtain ring combined with metal buttons. A belt is made from machine made cords by the five strand plaited braid method. Lower left to right. Left - divided head threaded with beads and worked in detached buttonhole stitch. Second from left - three strand plaited braid made into a loop and wrapped at the neck. Third from left - a Basic Tassel No. 2 with a shorter overskirt topped with a decorative bead and detached buttonhole plastic ring. Fourth from left - a Basic Tassel No.2 was first cut at the bottom and threaded through a buckle and an overskirt added. The rest are different variations of the flower tassel with fringed ends and machine made cords.

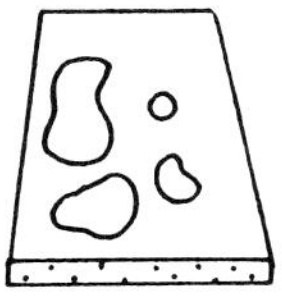
Fig.5a

Moulds - creating sculptured relief with fomecore – Photo page 35 and Figure 5

To create sculptured shapes for tassels, box lids or any other use proceed as follows:-

1. Draw the desired shape onto the card.
2. Then draw concentrically smaller shapes onto the card, repeating the shape of the first. Refer Figure 5a. Score the shape with a sharp Stanley or craft knife and cut through the fomecore.
3. The edges can then be bevelled or slanted.
4. Glue the shapes in place with craft glue, one on top of the other. The edges may be further trimmed and bevelled until the desired shape is achieved. Refer Figure 5b.

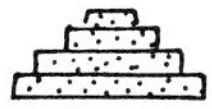
Fig.5b

When cutting straight edges use a metal ruler to guide the knife. This mould can then be covered with any type of fabric, suede or fine leather and secured with glue or by lacing with a needle and sewing cotton. Refer Figure 5c.

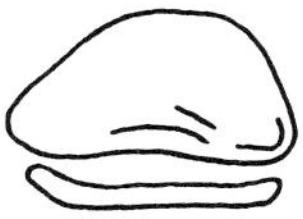
Fig.5c

5. The back may be concealed by embroidery stitches or by glueing another piece of fabric or covered card. Refer Figure 5d.

The use of this mould is dictated by laundering requirements.

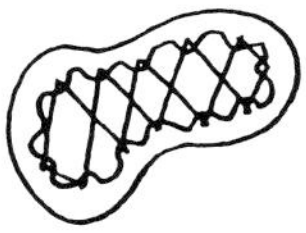
Fig.5d

Decorative tassel heads

Many varieties of decorative tassel heads are described where shown throughout the book.

Decorative tassel skirts

Apart from the straight skirt made by a basic tassel there are several variations which create surprising results.

Overskirts

Method A – Photo page 46

1. Make Basic Tassel No. 2 to create the body of this tassel.
2. To make the overskirt use another card template the length of the measurement from the neck to the bottom of the skirt.
3. Measure the distance around the neck of the skirt and mark this in pencil at the top of the card pattern.
4. Wind yarn around the card for the width of 3 above. Wrap plenty of yarn to create a good, full overskirt. I usually wrap about the same number of times as the body of the tassel, say seventy-five to one hundred times. Wrap twice as many for a fuller skirt.
5. With a separate piece of strong yarn equal to 4 ply crochet or No. 5 or 8 coton perle, take double back stitches .6 mm (.25 in) long across the top of the card, securing at both ends.

6. Slip the overskirt off the card and tie it firmly around the neck of the tassel with a reef knot.
7. The overskirt may be cut or left in loops.

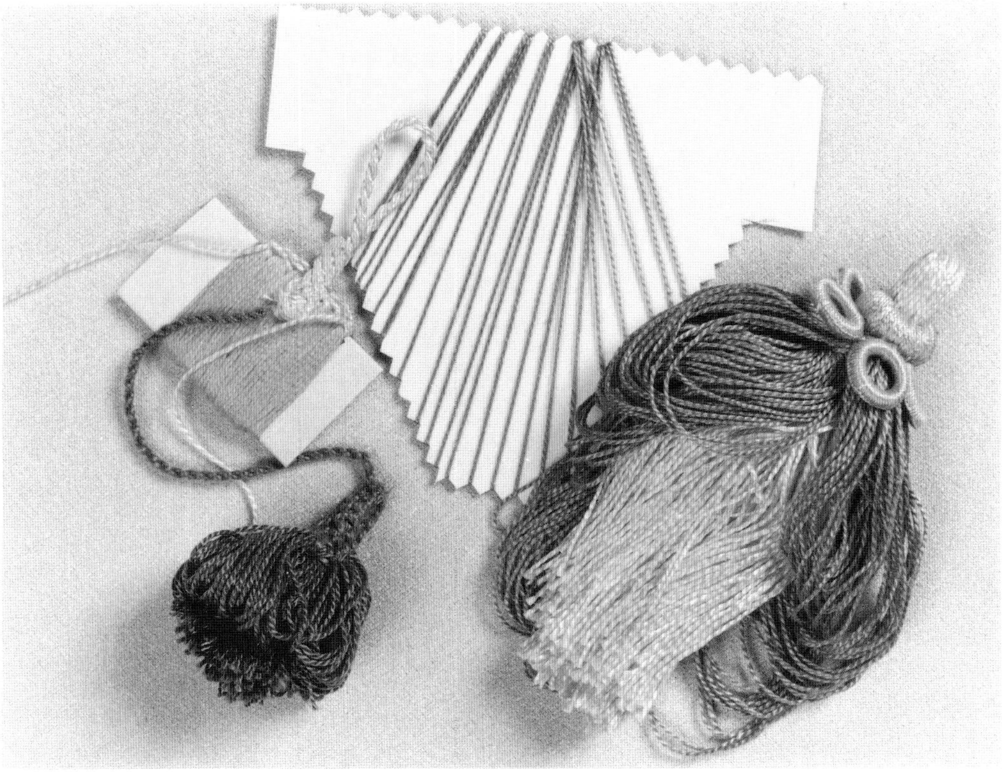

Shaped overskirt. Left – a card template is shown with the holding cord in place and two rows of detached buttonhole at the top ready to be tied around the holding cord to make the fuchsia tassel shown below it. Right – card template for shaped overskirt ready to be wound with yarn. Next to it is the finished overskirt tied to a basic tassel which has a vertically wrapped neck decorated with plastic rings covered with detached buttonhole stitch.

Fuchsia tassel – Plate X

For a fine fuchsia tassel use No. 8 coton perle or 20 crochet cotton equivalent. A thicker effect is made with No. 5 coton perle or 4 ply crochet equivalent. Other effects can be achieved using ribbon, cord, bubbly yarn - in fact any yarn may be used to create a simple but beautiful tassel by following steps 1 to 5 of method A but adding the following:-

1. Work two rows of detached buttonhole stitch on top of the double back stitch to secure and allow neat joining to the body of the tassel. Refer photo above.
2. Take the looped skirt off the card and tie firmly around the neck of the tassel with a reef knot.
3. Then take detached buttonhole stitches between the top of the skirt and the neck to secure the skirt in place.

I use the following measurements for fuchsia tassels:-

a. Body - 4 cm (1.5 in) long - wind seventy-five to two hundred times around card - cut the bottom of the skirt; Overskirt - 2.5 cm (1 in) - no less than one hundred and sixty times around card - leave uncut;

b. Vary the skirt of the tassel to 3 cm (1.25 in) or 2 cm (.75 in) and still winding no less than one hundred and sixty times around card.

Pendant loops – Plate X

Another version of method A is to make one or more looped skirts and sew them around a thick cord which is used as a foundation and not seen. Attach a holding cord to the top in proportion to the thickness of the tassel.

The top of the pendant loops can then be decorated with rings or covered wire.

Shaped overskirts – Plate X and Photo page 46

1. To create a shaped skirt make a card template, with the angle pointing down being quite acute in order to gain a noticeable variation in the length of the skirt. Pinking shears are good for making a jagged edge on the card.
2. Double back stitch across the top as in method A.
3. If leaving the loops uncut remove the tassel by tearing the card piece by piece. If the skirt is to be cut then the tassel may be cut off the card.
4. Tie the skirt to the neck of the tassel.

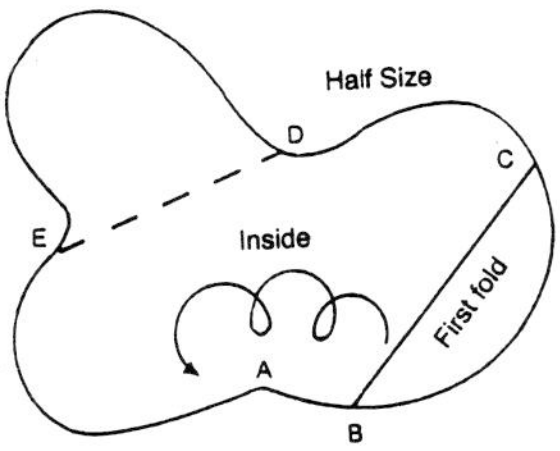

Fig. 6

Rolled overskirts - Leather or felt – Plate VIII and Figure 6

1. Trace the shape in Figure 6 and make a card template which gives no seam allowance as it is not necessary for this procedure.
2. Cut a piece of fabric in this shape. Suitable fabrics are non fraying such as felt, suede and leather. A different coloured lining may be made by cutting out a second shape and bonding or glueing it to the first.
3. To roll the shape, first place a small amount of craft or fabric glue near A and lay the holding cord across A-D.
4. With A to form the top of the skirt make the first fold B-C around the holding cord then continue rolling in the direction of the arrow.
5. Glue or stitch the last fold in place.

6. To create a different effect commence folding at D-E so that the top of the shape forming the hole is made at D.

7. The shape may be made larger or smaller to suit the purpose.

Rolled overskirt - fabric

A rolled skirt in the same shape as leather or felt above may be made in fraying fabric as follows:-

1. Cut two pieces of fabric leaving a small seam allowance. To stiffen the shape a third layer of interlining may be added.

2. With right sides of the fabric together machine stitch around the edge leaving a gap approximately 2.5 cm (1 in).

3. Turn the shape right side out through the gap and press. Sew the gap closed with ladder stitch.

Flared overskirt – Plate VIII

Detached buttonhole stitch is first worked over the head and then from the neck outwards to form a peplum skirt.

Free machine embroidered lace may be sewn on to create a similar effect.

Flower tassel – Plate IX, Photo page 44, Photo page 49 and Figure 7

Flower tassels can be made from a piece of 10 cm (4 in) square fabric.

1. Fold the fabric in two and stitch the long ends together 6 mm (.25 in) from the edge to produce a cylinder.

2. Fold the cylinder in half with the seam concealed between the fold.

3. Attach the cylinder to a cord by gathering in the raw edges of the fabric and stitching to the cord. Refer to Figure 7.

4. Pull the cylinder down over the join. Beads, French knots and bullion knots may be attached to the bottom of the cord.

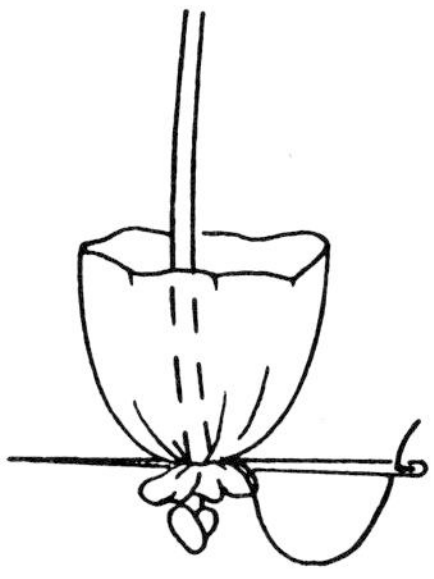

Fig. 7

Variations of this method are:-

a. Change the width and length of the fabric.

b. Stitch two or more on top of each other.

Fabric tassels

Embroidery skills are an asset when making these delightfully different baubles for use on their own or to finish off embroidered items such as cushions, bags, clothing.

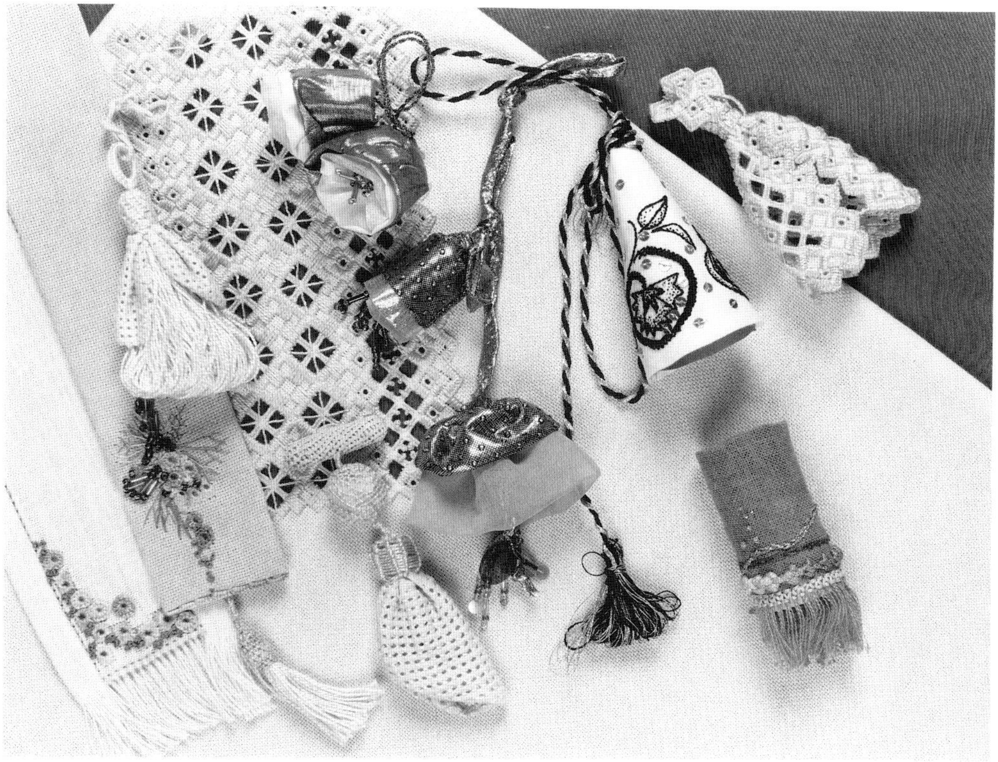

Flower and fabric tassels and bookmarks. Left - embroidered bookmark with a fringed edge of foursided stitch. Second from left - embroidered and tasselled bookmark with a scalloped edge of detached buttonhole stitch. On top of this bookmark is a pulled thread tassel worked in four-sided stitch. Third from left - flower tassels with beaded centres. Second from right - blackwork tassel worked on linen. Right - fabric tassel worked in Hardangar embroidery. The background fabric is also worked in Hardangar embroidery. Bottom left - pulled thread fabric tassel with a head of back stitch woven web stitch topped with a ball of quilt wadding and a dowel plug covered in detached buttonhole stitch. Bottom right - cylindrical tassel, worked on dyed fabric the fringed edge is worked in three sided stitch above which is raised chain band, chain stitch and French knots.

A. **Hardangar tassel** – Photo above

First work Hardangar embroidery on a rectangle approximately 13 cm (5.2 in) wide by 9 cm (3.5 in) long leaving 12 mm (.5 in) seam allowance at the top of the rectangle. When the embroidery is complete gather the fabric at the top in yarn equal to 4 ply crochet cotton or No.5 coton perle, wrapping the yarn around the top for 12 mm (.5 in) to secure and create a padded foundation for the detached buttonhole stitch to be worked over the head. A motif of embroidered linen may also be added at the top of the tassel.

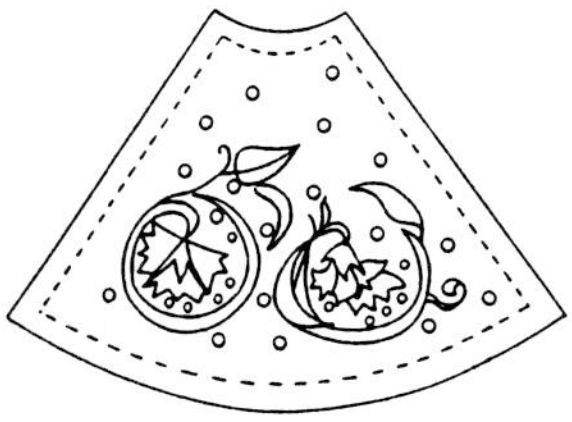

Fig. 8
Quarter size

B. Blackwork tassel – Photo page 49 and Figure 8

1. Embroider blackwork onto a cone shape of linen, as shown in Figure 8, in black coton perle No. 8 or 2 strands embroidery floss and gold embroidery thread.
2. Trim around the cone shape leaving a 6 mm (.25 in) seam allowance on all sides.
3. Cut out a piece of iron-on interfacing the exact size of the cone shape without seam allowance, and fuse the two shapes together by pressing with a warm iron.
4. Press the seam allowance over onto the interfacing.
5. Hand stitch a lining onto the back.
6 Join the side seam with ladder stitch.

C. Pulled thread tassel – Photo page 49

Embroider a rectangle of even weave linen 13 cm (5.2 in) wide by 9 cm (3.5 in) long with four sided stitch. When the embroidery is complete gather the fabric at the top in strong yarn equal to 4 ply crochet or No.5 coton perle, wrapping the yarn around the top for 12 mm (.5 in) to secure and to create a padded foundation for the detached buttonhole stitch to be worked over the head.

D. Triangular tasselled jewellery and trimmings with beads and embroidery – Plate IX and Photo page 52

Three equilateral triangles with one point cut off form each triangular tassel. The triangles shown on Plate IX and Photo page 52 are 3 cm (1.2 in) and 2 cm (.8 in) on each side. An easy way to make the triangles is to buy isometric graph paper which is divided into triangles. Glue a sheet of this graph paper to medium weight card - greeting cards are a good weight. Cut out the triangles to the desired size with a Stanley or craft knife. If the triangular tassels are to be laundered cut the shapes out of plastic. Trim a wedge off one corner. Proceed as follows to dress the card or plastic templates:-

1. Cut out fabric leaving a 6 mm (.25 in) seam allowance all around the shape.

2. Fold the fabric over the edges and lace them together with needle and sewing cotton at the back of the card, turning the corners under neatly with the needle.
3. Join the three shapes together at the seams with ladder stitch. The edges with the trimmed points should all meet at the same end. Leave the third and final join until beads and stitchery have been worked on the back, over the lacing threads and the seam allowance.
4. Embroider the inside with bullion knots and beads.
5. Ladder stitch the third join. Any untidy edges can be covered with beads and stitches.

E. **Cylindrical, embroidered tassel on dyed fabric** – Photo page 49

Hand dyed fabric, fringe held in place with three-sided stitch. Embroider linen and then join side seam with ladder stitch. Insert a card cylinder or a rolled piece of paper to hold the shape.

Dyeing to be different – Plates IV and XIII

Colourful and different tassels can be made by dyeing your own yarn or painting it with fabric paint.

Space dyeing with different colours on one length of yarn is very attractive.

There are many books on dyeing and these contain detailed instructions. Two ways to go about space dyeing yarns to obtain unique effects are:-

1. Wrap the yarn to be dyed around a card pattern, tie the loops together at the top and the bottom, remove the card pattern and then space dye starting with one colour or tone at one end and another colour or tone at the other.
2. Make up a whole tassel and then dye it or apply fabric paint.

   Space dyed yarn is very attractive when used to wrap beads and shapes as shown in photo page 35, and the beads hanging from the tassel in plate XVI.

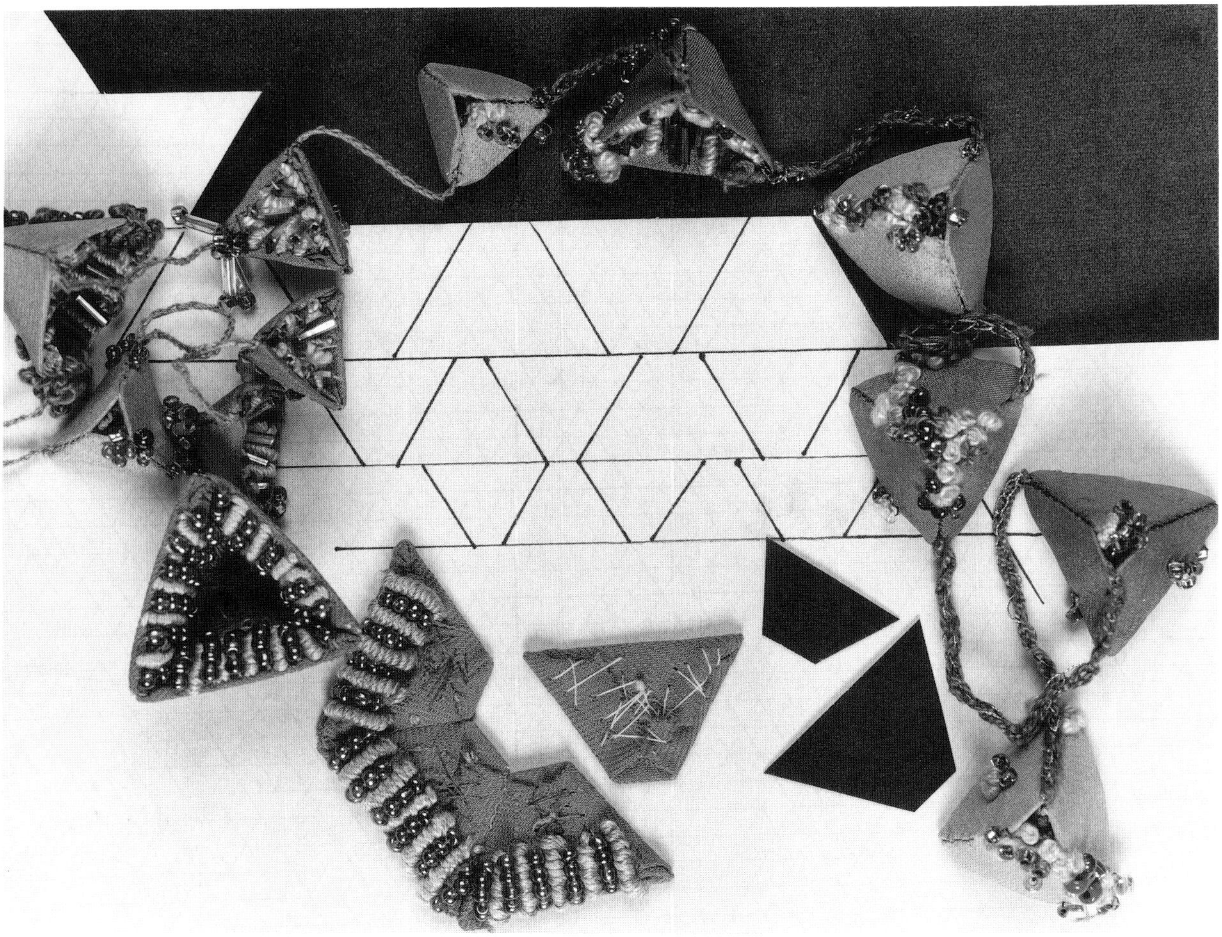

Triangular tassels. Three card shapes are covered with fabric, embroidered with beads and bullion knot stitch then joined together to make one triangular tassel.

Chapter 3

Cords and Braids

Frogging

Photo page 54 shows frogging made from rouleaux cord with a thick purchased cord threaded through it to give body. Choose a design which forms a continuous curved line. The button is made from a Josephine looped knot pulled tightly and stitched in place.

To apply the frogging lay the fabric to which the frogging is to be sewn onto a pinboard. Pin the rouleaux cord onto the fabric in the selected design concealing the seamline of the rouleaux cord. Stitch in place.

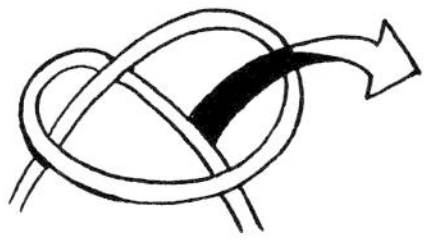

Fig. 9a

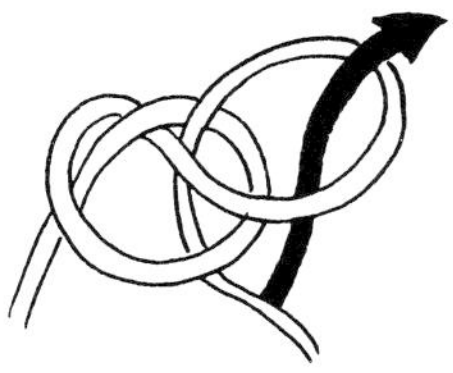

Fig. 9b

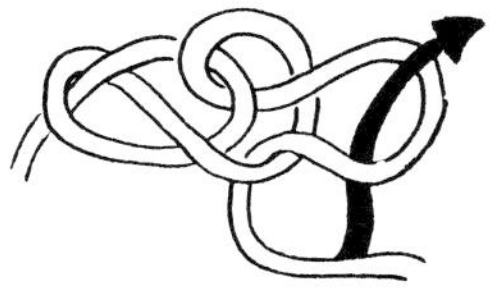

Fig. 9c

Knotted or braided finger cords – Figure 9 and Photo page 55

In knotting ropecraft this is also known as Drummer Boy's Plait and is made with one strand of yarn or cording.

1. As shown in Figure 9a form a loop and pin it onto a pinboard or tie it to a hook.

2. Form another loop as in Figure 9b.

Keep on repeating 2 above - Figure 9c.

Machine wrapped cord – Photo page 56

With zigzag stitch the widest width and the desired stitch length sew together lengths of yarn which form the core. The number of lengths of yarn is determined by the thickness required and how many are able to be stitched together. Five strands of four ply crochet or No. 5 perle equivalent work well. Combine different textures as well as shiny and dull yarn to make different effects.

To create different types of effects the zigzag stitches can be wide apart to reveal the core or very close satin stitching. Close satin stitching may be varied by leaving unworked spaces between blocks of satin stitching.

Needlewoven

Chapter 6 shows how to work needleweaving to make the following cords:-

- detached buttonhole
- alternating detached buttonhole
- twisted detached buttonhole
- woven - plain weave
- wrapping

Rouleaux cords – Photo below

Rouleaux cording is made from strips of fabric cut on the bias. The width of the bias strip varies depending on the required finished thickness. I usually use 24 mm (1 in) wide bias strips to make a finished rouleaux cord 6mm (.25 in) wide.

Fold the fabric in half, wrong sides together, and machine stitch 6 mm (.25 in) from the folded edge. This tube is pulled back through itself with either a loop turner or a strong yarn attached to one end of the fabric and threaded double through a knitter's needle. Another method is to attach a thick cord at one end and pull it through, leaving it there to give body to the cord, particularly when making frogging.

Coloured shadows are created by threading space dyed or multi-coloured yarns through a rouleaux cord made from white organza.

Lovely effects are made when the yarn causes the cord to gather in curves and frills.

Rouleaux cords, padded – Photo page 63

Rouleaux cords made from 6 cm (2.5 in) bias fabric strips padded with quilt wadding make a round roll like a sausage which can be plaited to make belts, rings and curtain tie-backs.

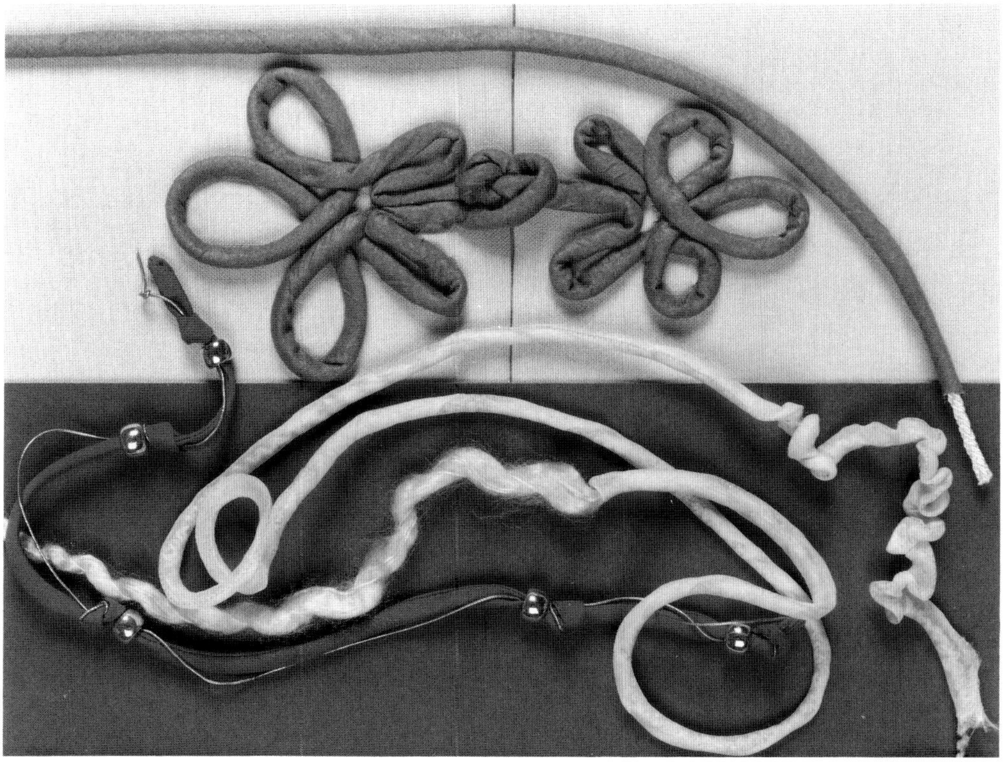

Frogging and rouleaux cords. The top half of the photo shows a trimming called frogging made from rouleaux cord threaded with cording. The bottom half shows rouleaux cords made from organza fabric and threaded with multi coloured bubbly wool and allowed to gather. A silk rouleaux is combined with metallic cord and beads.

To stop the wadding from catching in the sewing machine stabilise the fabric with a strip of tear-away fabric stabiliser which is removed following stitching or use a lightweight fabric such as organza which may be trimmed after stitching and left in the padded roll.

Twisted cords – Photo page 56

Any kind of yarn and metal thread is suitable for inclusion in twisted cords. Experiment with each yarn to see the effects and thickness created. If a twisted cord is too thin multiply the number of yarns before tying.

A different type of cord is created by re-twisting together two previously twisted cords.

Twisted cords by hand

1. Take a length of yarn approximately eight times the desired finished length.

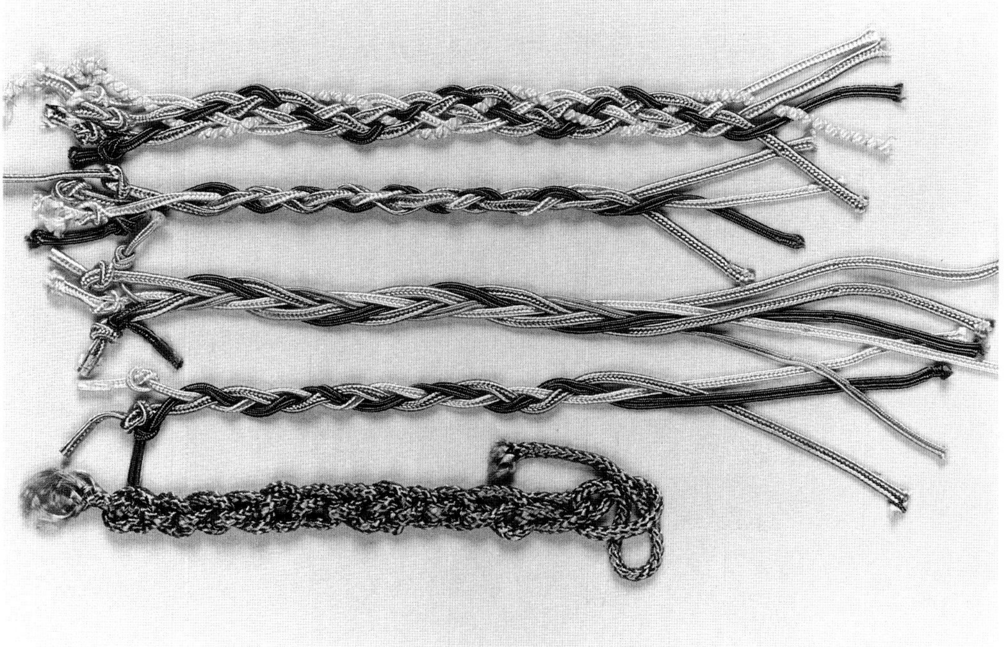

Cords - hand made. Top row - knotted or braided finger cord. Second row - three strand braid. Third row - five strand plaited braid. Fourth row - four strand round braid. Fifth row - five strand flat braid.

2. Double it by hooking it over a door knob or door key.
3. Twist the doubled cord between thumb and index finger until it is tightly coiled.
4. Find the half way point, carefully double the cord and let it twist in small sections to prevent knotting. When making a very long

twisted cord I hook it to a wardrobe key and place a chair at the half way point to stabilise the coiled yarn. Should you require a lot of shorter cords of the same yarn make up a long twisted cord and cut the required lengths between two overhand knots 24 mm (1 in) apart. The knots prevent the cord unravelling when it is cut.

Twisted holding cords

An easy way to twist the holding cord at the end of the tassel is to first secure the tassel to a surface with a pin - an ironing board cover is suitable. Twist the yarn in two groups in the same direction.

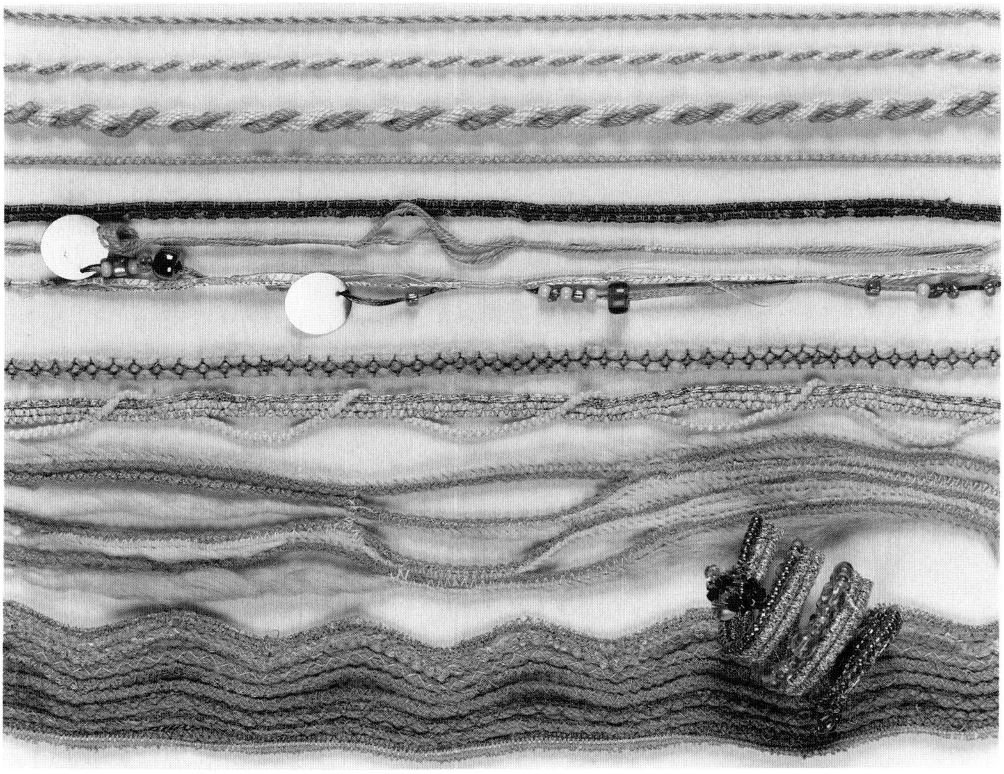

Cords - twisted and machine made braids. Top - using two strands 4 ply crochet yarn. Second row - using two cords of above. Third row - using twelve strands 4 ply crochet yarn. Fourth row - Basic machine wrapped cord - zigzag stitch over six strands 4 ply crochet yarn, widest stitch - length 2. Fifth row - two machine wrapped cords joined together side by side with decorative machine feather stitch to create a Russia type braid. Sixth row - random machine satin stitching over five strands of 4 ply crochet yarn. Seventh row - random machine stitching over various yarns, metallic cord and ribbon cord threaded with beads. Eighth row - two machine wrapped cords joined with a decorative machine diamond stitch. Ninth row - braid of three basic machine made cords joined together then interlaced with a fourth cord which is then machine stitched in place. Tenth row - different types of yarn and cords joined randomly to create an original braid of open work. This type of openwork braid is ideal for use as insertions to create a lacy effect. Eleventh row - zigzag braid. On top of the zigzag braid is a scarf ring made of Russia type braid stitched with wire. It is then hand stitched to a wire threaded with beads and twisted over a cylindrical shape to form the spiral effect.

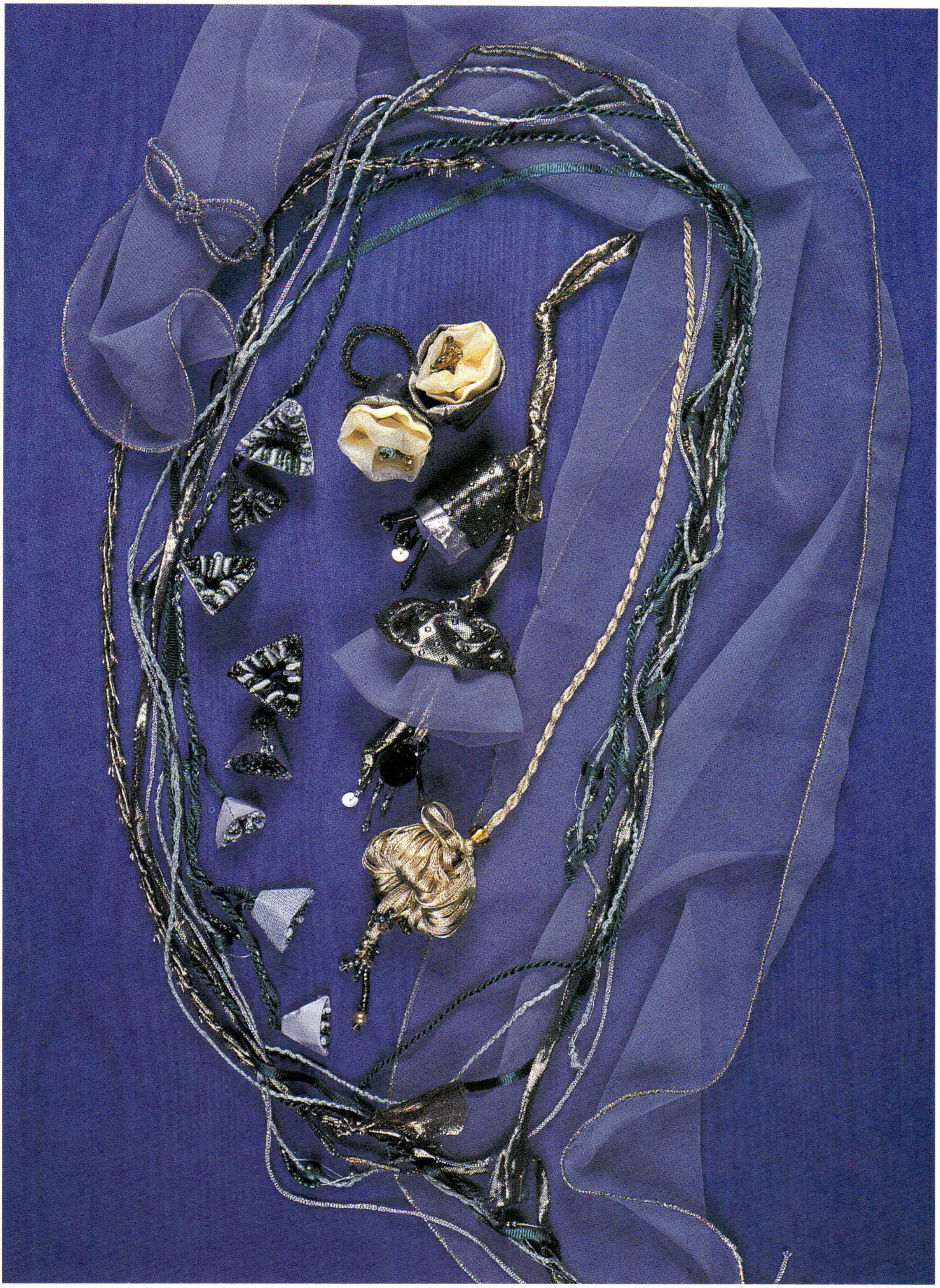

Plate IX

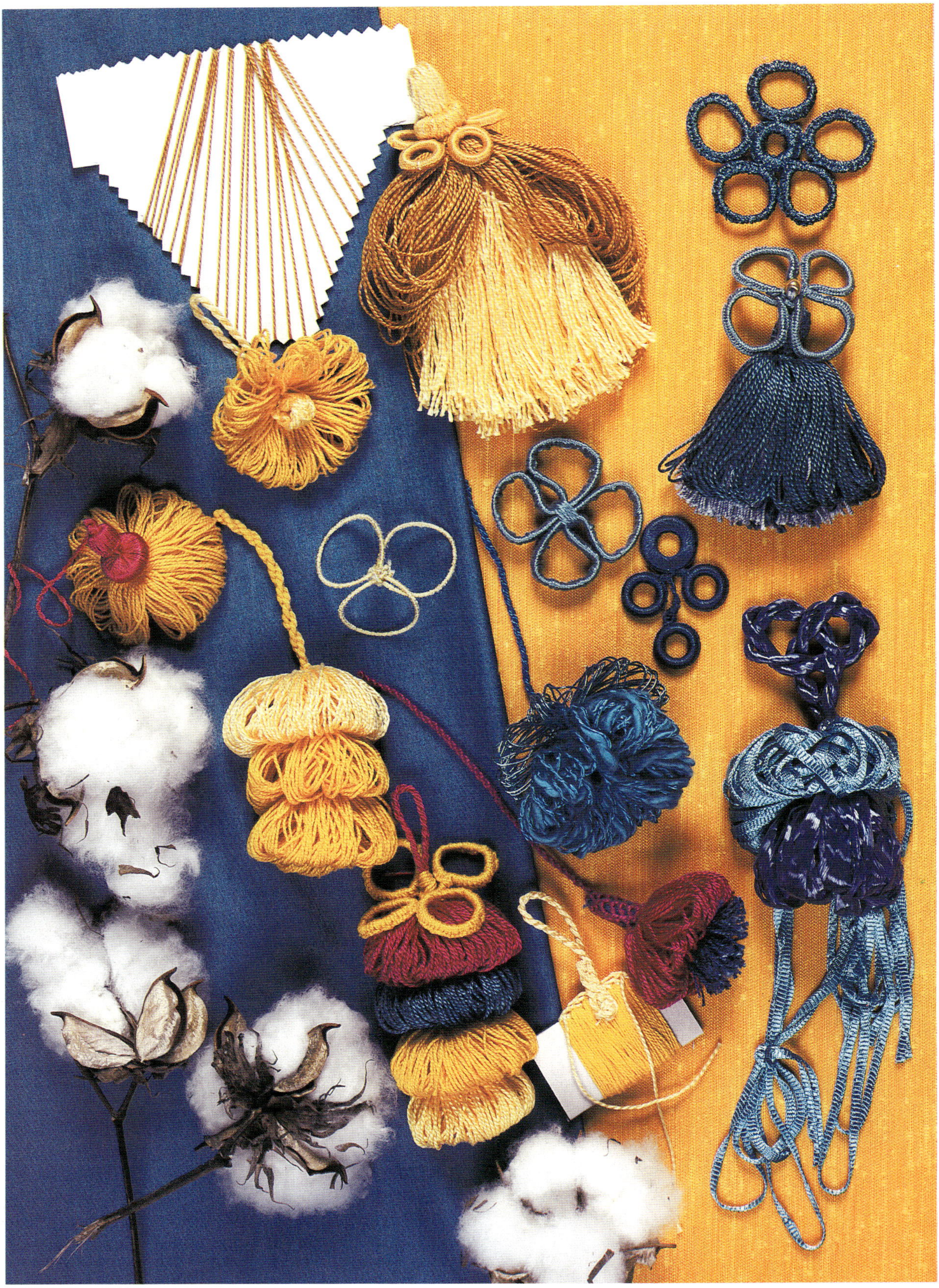

Plate X

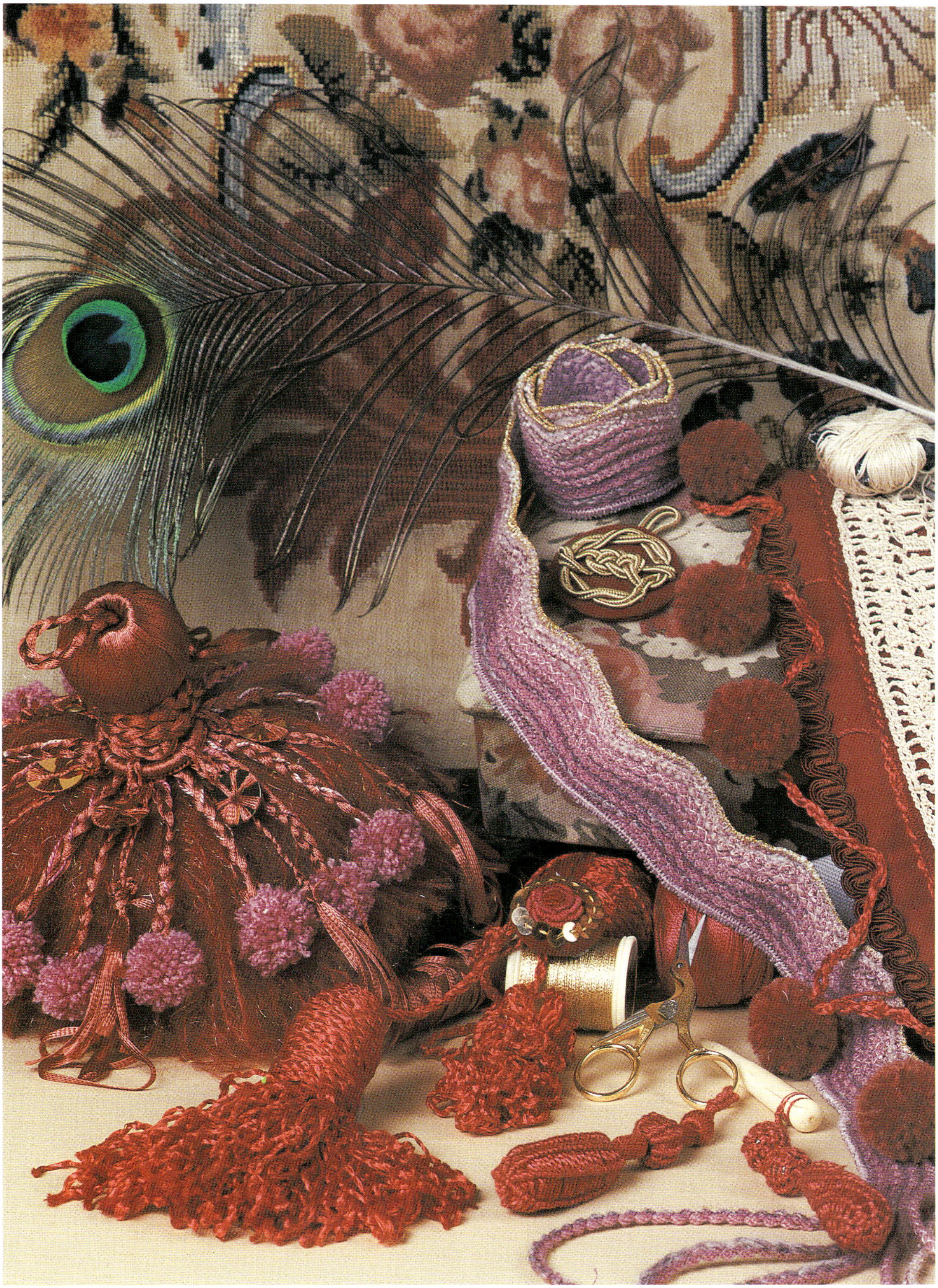

Plate XI

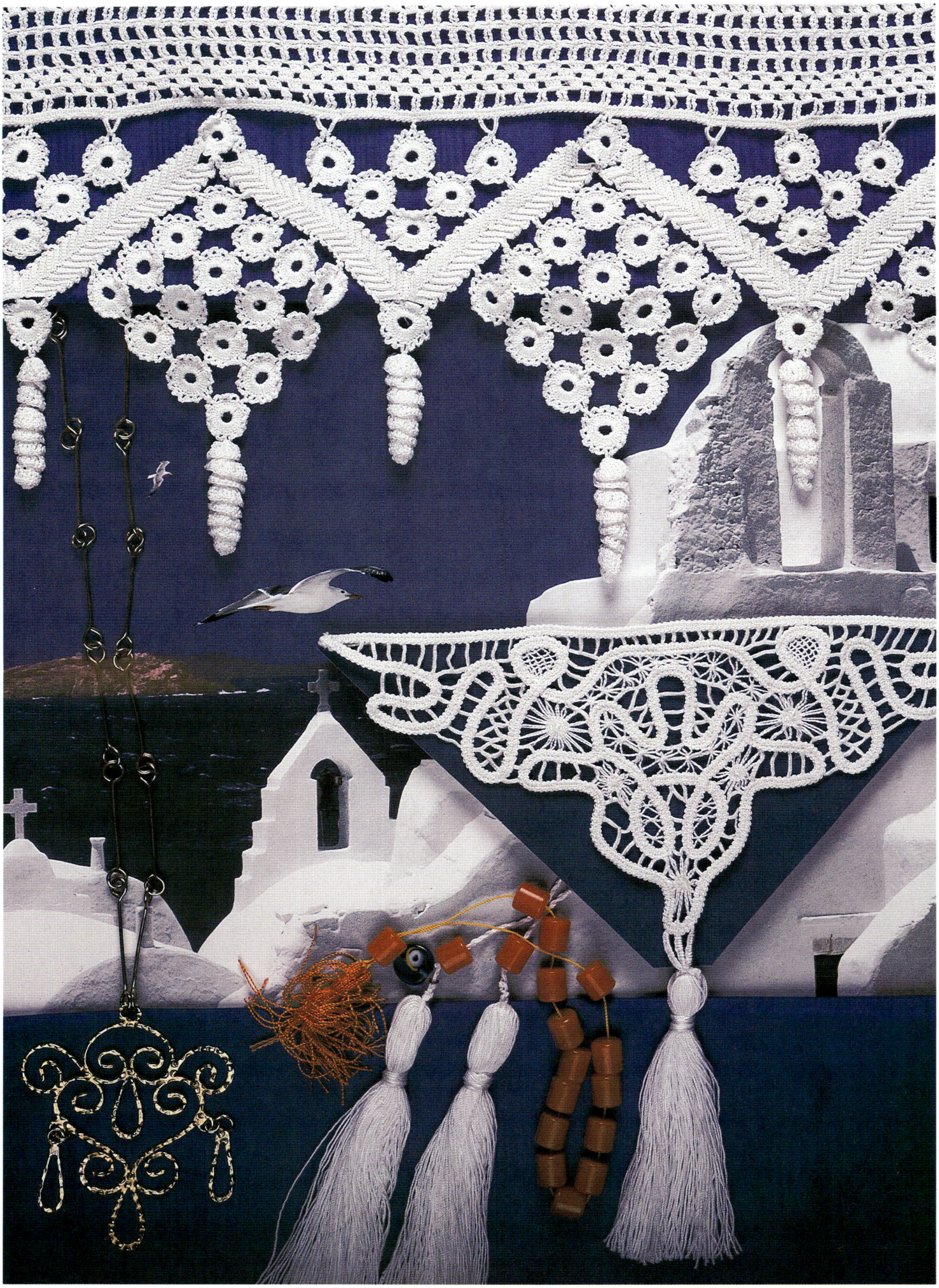

Plate XII

Plate IX Triangular Jewellery
A scarf ring made of machine stitched Russia type braid is tied in a square decorative knot. Various machine made cords include twisted strips of frayed gold fabric, knitting ribbon and machine made cords which were strung with beads prior to machine stitching. The triangular tassels are covered card or plastic which are then embroidered with bullion knots in embroidery yarn and beads. The triangular shapes may be varied by joining only two instead of three triangles as shown in the two lower triangular tassels. The row of flower tassels down the centre shows multiple layered skirts held by rouleaux cording and decorated inside with French knots and beads. The bottom tassel is a fuchsia tassel made from fine rayon ribbon.

Plate X Cotton on Blue
The fuchsia tassel is featured with many variations including two, three and four fuchsia tassels joined to form pendant loops. The top left hand corner shows the card template for shaped overskirts and the tassel to its right features a shaped overskirt with detached buttonhole plastic rings forming a collar. Directly under this tassel is a flower shape which is made of two plastic milk bottle top rings covered in detached buttonhole and sewn into place as shown. To the left of this flower shape is a triple ring shape which is made of machine zigzag stitched wire twisted into the shape and hand stitched in place. The top right shows an arrangement of soft detached buttonhole rings. Beneath it a fuchsia tassel features a flower shape made of wire covered with detached buttonhole stitch. In the centre at the bottom, just above the cotton boll is a card template showing the preparation for a fuchsia tassel with two rows of detached buttonhole stitch securing the top of the wound yarn and a looped cord stitched in place ready for the looped skirt to be tied around it.

Plate XI Victoriana
Back row Left - The Madame Pompadour tassel is a combination of many pieces. The skirt is made of mohair knitting yarn covered with an overskirt of pom poms and sequins attached to three-strand braided cords made from rayon ribbon and joined to a detached buttonhole curtain ring. The neck is wrapped with the braided cording. The head is a painted polystyrene ball with a hole pierced through the middle allowing it to be wrapped with the same ribbon as the cording. Middle - Zigzag braid made with machine made cords. Sitting on the box in front of the rolled braid is a covered button with a Josephine knot made from purchased Russia braid. This could also be made with machine made Russia type braid. Right - A red suede cloth is fringed with purchased braid and pom poms attached to twisted cords. Front row Left - Rayon yarn is made into a twisted cord and affixed to a plastic curtain rod end used as a mould to form the head of this tassel. To the right and slightly behind this tassel is a machine made fringed swirl attached to a covered button mould decorated with bullion knot stitch rose and stitched sequins. The stork scissors are tagged with three covered and embellished shapes. Closest to the scissors handle is a wrapped jug bead; below it is a wooden bead worked with back stitch webbing; below it is a wrapped 'bead' cut from plastic tubing; the long cylindrical shape at the end is a fabric covered, padded wooden dowel plug which has been further embellished with back stitch web stitch. In the bottom right hand corner an embroidery tool known as an 'awl' or 'stiletto' and used to make holes in fabric is also tagged with a similar arrangement to the scissors tag except the shapes are worked in detached buttonhole stitch.

Plate XII Greek Curtain
A crocheted window curtain, more than fifty years old, is trimmed with crocheted swirls. A triangle of needlewoven lace is attached to a rectangle of cotton fabric to trim a little wooden shelf. Both were worked by the late Mrs Ipapanti Zouroudis from the island of Simi, Greece. Basic Tassel No. 1 makes up the three tassels at the bottom of the page while three bands of detached buttonhole needleweaving attaches one tassel to the needlewoven lace.

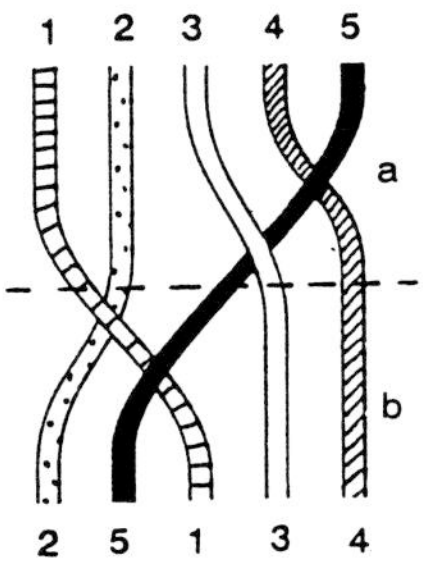

Fig. 10

Tie the two groups together with an overhand knot. Unpin the tassel, allowing the two groups of yarn to twist together by dangling the tassel. This method makes a very tidy connection between the tassel and the holding cord as there is no stitching involved.

Twisted cords by machine – Photo page 56

The sewing machine offers a wide variety of quick ways to make cords and braids.

Tie the yarn to an empty bobbin, place it on the bobbin winder and slowly work the machine. Follow step 4 as in hand made cords. For long cords a second person is required to assist.

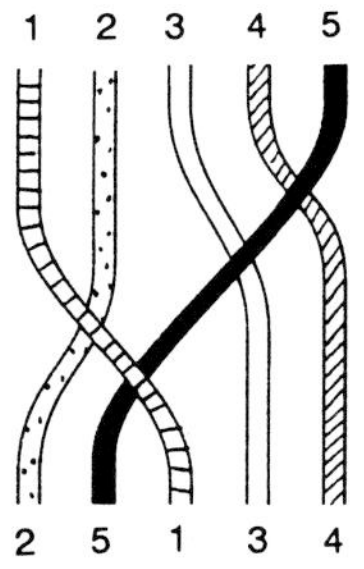

Fig. 11

Braids

Five strand flat braid – Photo page 55 and Figure 10

Figures 10a and b show the two steps required to make this flat braid which is pinned to a soft board or tied to a hook during working.

1. Take the outside right cord over and under to the centre.
2. Take the outside left cord over and under to the centre.

Repeat these two steps.

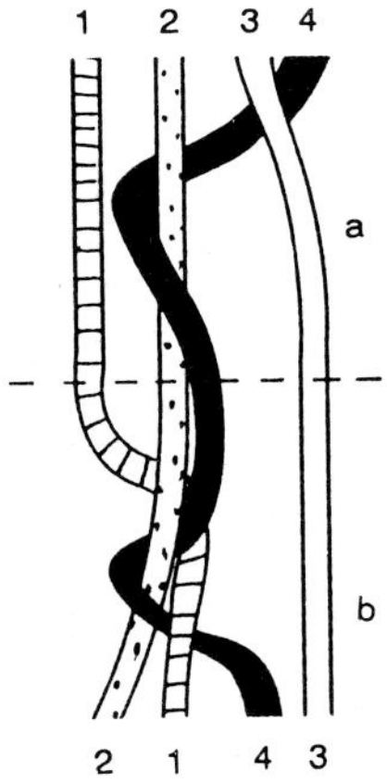

Fig. 12

Five strand plaited braid – Photo page 55 and Figure 11

Figure 11 shows the two steps required to make this plaited braid which is pinned to a soft board or tied to a hook during working.

1. Take the outside right cord over two to the centre.
2. Take the outside left cord over two to the centre.

Four strand round braid – Photo page 55 and Figure 12

Figures 12a and b show how to work this braid which is also best worked pinned to a soft board or tied to a hook.

1. Take the outside right cord behind and around the inner left.
2. Take the outside left cord behind and around the inner right.

Repeat. Twist and tighten the cords as you work.

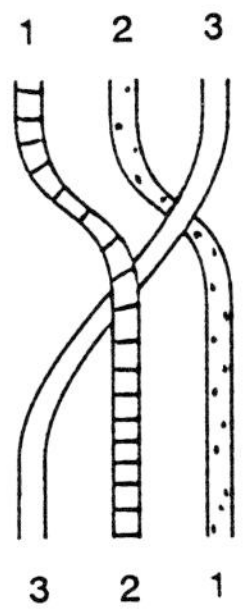

Fig. 13

Three strand braid – Photo page 55 and Figure 13

Most are familiar with this simple but effective braid shown in Figure 13.

1. Take the outside right cord to the centre.
2. Take the outside left cord to the centre. — Repeat.

Zigzag braid – Plate XI and Photo page 56

This braid is made in two steps. Cords need to be made first as follows.

Make approximately eight thick cords of graduating colours to achieve a finished width of 3.5 cm (1.25 in).

The cords are then made into a braid as follows:-

1. On a strip of interfacing or firm non-fraying fabric draw a zigzag line, the points being 5 cm (2 in) apart and dropping 1 cm (.5 in) to create the zigzag. If the interfacing is white and gaps appear as you complete the next step, the interfacing may be fabric painted first or touched up after.
2. With the widest zigzag stitch and No. 2 stitch length stitch the first cord in place on the zigzag line.
3. Stitch the rest of the cords parallel to the first.
4. Trim the edges of the braid to 6 mm (.25 in) and zigzag stitch once or twice to finish off the edge.

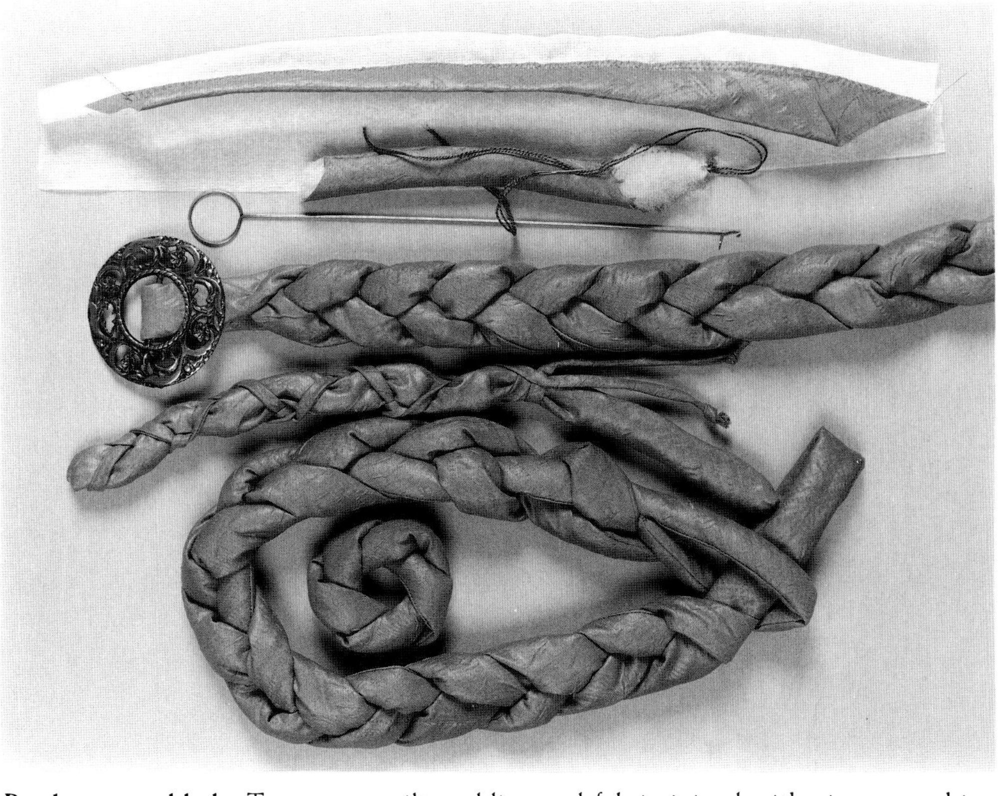

Rouleaux, padded. Top row - quilt wadding and fabric joined with zigzag machine stitching. Second row - shows the cord pulled through itself with a threaded needle or a loop turner. Third row - three strand braid makes a belt. Fourth row - three strand braid made from two strands of narrow unpadded rouleaux and one strand of padded rouleaux cords. Fifth row - three strand braid made into a curtain tie and decorative ring.

Chapter 4

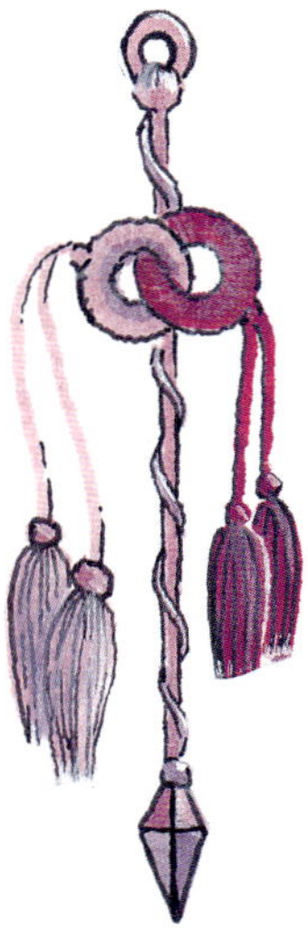

Fringing

Embroidered, Braided and Tasselled

Photo page 65 shows an edge embroidered in chain stitch, with the horizontal threads withdrawn to create a fringe. The remaining vertical threads are then plaited by the three strand braid method and a tassel is attached to the end of each braid.

Fringed swirls – Plate XI and Photo page 67

1. Wrap yarn horizontally around a hairpin crochet hook as shown in photo page 67.
2. Wrap the yarn once or twice vertically down the centre or to one side of the horizontal wrapping.
3. Machine zigzag over the vertical wrapping once or twice to secure.
4. Remove the wrapping and twist the swirl into place.
5. The swirls may be cut or left in loops.

Fringed tassel by hand – Plate IV and Photo page 67

1. Cut out a card template approximately 18 cm (7 in) long and 33 mm (1.25 in) wide.
2. Wind yarn around card twenty or thirty times for finer No. 8 coton perle or No. 20 crochet equivalent, or 15-25 times for 4 ply crochet or No.5 coton perle equivalent. These numbers are varied to suit the thickness of yarn and the desired result. Do not cut yarn.
3. Take yarn approximately 25 mm (1 in) away from the first group and wind another group the same number of times. Do not cut yarn.
4. Repeat 3 above until the card template is full, about eight groups.
5. To join the groups of yarn thread a needle with double yarn and tie each group with two or three detached buttonhole stitches.
6. Between each group make a cord by tying knotted or braided finger cord.

7. When all groups of yarn are securely fastened and joined cut the bottom of the yarn with sharp scissors.
8. The fringing can then be attached as a tassel trim or attached to braid.

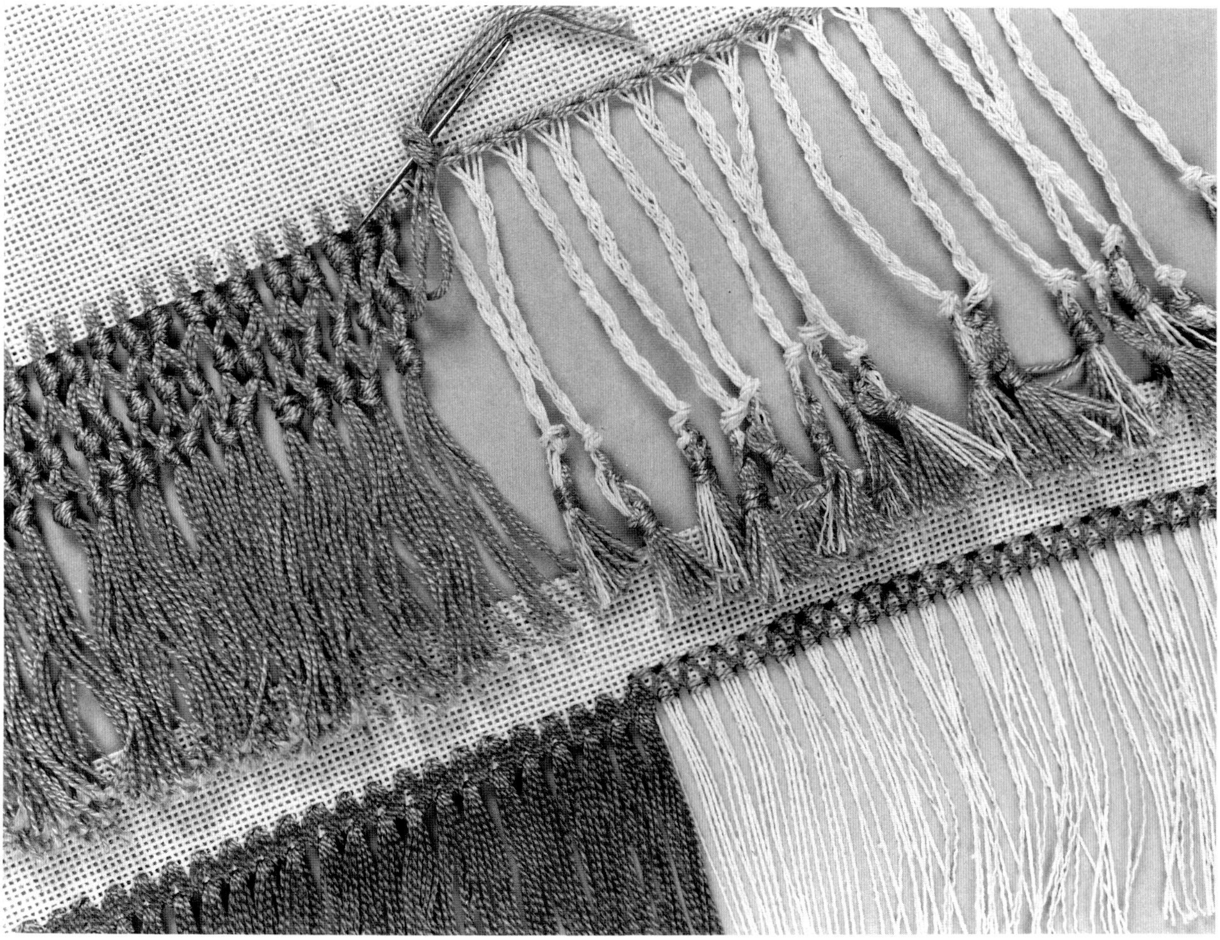

Fringes - hand made, have been worked on canvas to show the method of working. The two examples on the right show the fabric forming the fringe and these fringes work well with linen or cotton fabrics where the threads are easy to separate and remove. Top left - overhand knot fringe - worked in No. 5 coton perle - the knots are guided into position by using a needle as shown. Top right - a row of chain stitch secures the edge of the fabric before removing the horizontal weft threads. The remaining vertical warp threads have been plaited by the three strand braid method and tied with overhand knots. A tassel is stitched to the bottom of each braid. Bottom left - four lengths of No. 5 coton perle yarn have been threaded through the fabric and knotted by the lark's head knot method. The back of the lark's head knot creates a different effect thus the fringe is effective on both sides. Bottom right - a row of three sided stitch is worked on the fabric then the horizontal weft threads removed.

Fringed tassel by machine – Plate IV and Photo page 67

1. Using a firm piece of coathanger wire bent to a U shape work steps 2 to 4 inclusive as for hand fringed tassel. Clothes pegs may be used to prevent the yarn from slipping.
2. Take a cord or doubled yarn down the middle of the wire at a right angle to the horizontal threads.
3. Loop the cord firmly once around each group with an overhand knot.
4. Machine zigzag down the centre cord stitching backwards and forwards at each bundle of threads to secure.
5. Work steps 7 and 8 as for hand made fringed tassel.

Knotted, overhand fringe – Photo page 65

1. Cut lengths of yarn the same size.
2. Thread one or more lengths of yarn into a tapestry needle and thread through the edge of the fabric to be trimmed.
3. Tie the yarn into an overhand knot. It is helpful to use a needle as shown in photo page 65 to assist in the placement of the knots. This photo also shows that the lengths of yarn may be further knotted together as many times as desired.

Knotted, lark's head fringe

Photo page 65 shows this knot which is clearly illustrated in Figure 15 on page 69.

Pulled thread fringe

1. Work a row of three-sided stitch on open-weave fabric leaving fabric below the stitches for the fringe.
2. Remove the horizontal threads from the fabric leaving the vertical threads to create the fringe.

   Photo page 49 shows embroidered bookmarks and a cylindrical tassel with a pulled thread fringe. Photo page 65 clearly shows this fringe.

A similar fringe can also be worked with four sided stitch.

Twisted cord fringe for tassel skirts – Photo page 67

Tassel skirts can be made by the following method:-

1. Make a long twisted cord.
2. Wrap the cord around a pattern card in a single row for approximately 8 cm.

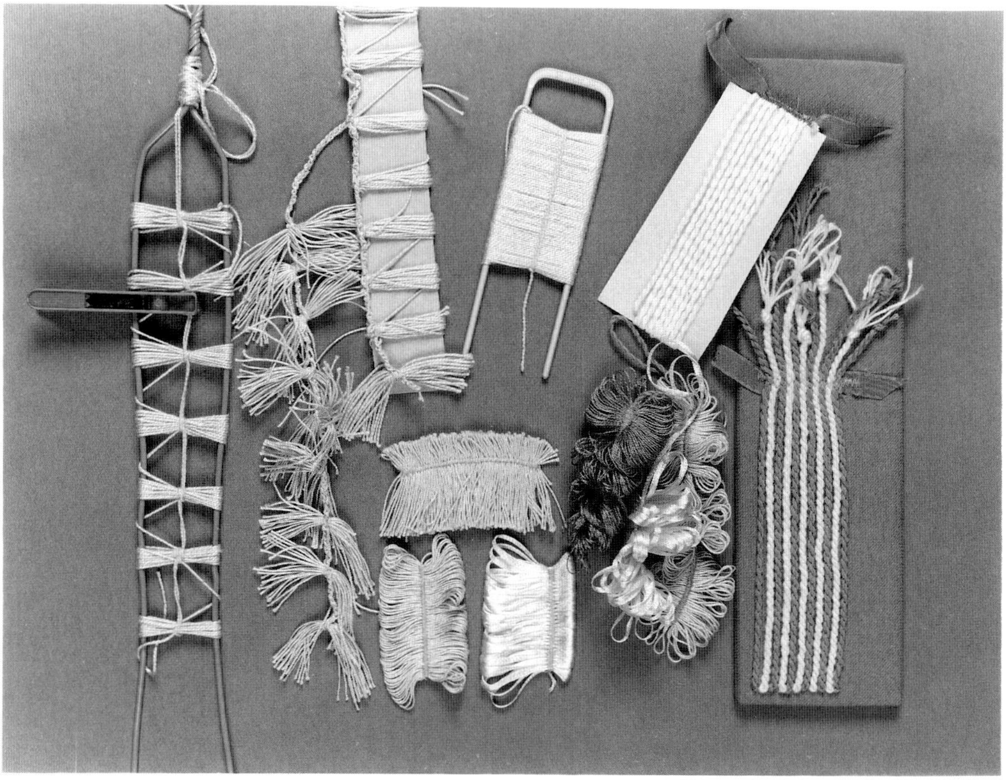

Fringes and fringed tassels. A coat hanger bent into shape shows the method of preparing wrapped yarn for a fringed tassel to be joined by machine. A card template is wrapped to show the method of making a fringed tassel to be joined by hand knotting method. The finished tassel is shown between these two templates. Top centre shows a hairpin crochet hook wrapped with yarn in preparation for machine stitching. Below the hook three different ways of making swirls are shown. After machine stitching the swirls are easily twisted into spirals. Second from the right – Bottom – a group of machine made swirls made in 4 ply crochet yarn, ribbon and coton perle No. 5. Top – a card template is wrapped with a twisted cord and machine stitched at the top to secure the top and form a fringe. Far right – twisted cord fringe – lengths of twisted cords are stitched together.

3. With a separate piece of yarn equal to 4 ply crochet or No. 5 coton perle, take double back stitches approximately 4 mm (1/8 in) long across the top of the card.
4. Slip the skirt off the card pattern and pin the top, at the row of backstitching, to a ribbon approximately 12 mm (.5 in) wide.
5. Stitch the fringe to the ribbon with machine zigzag.
6. Roll the ribbon into a coil and hand stitch together.
7. This now forms a tassel skirt of very serviceable cording.

The same type of skirt can be made with machine made cording.

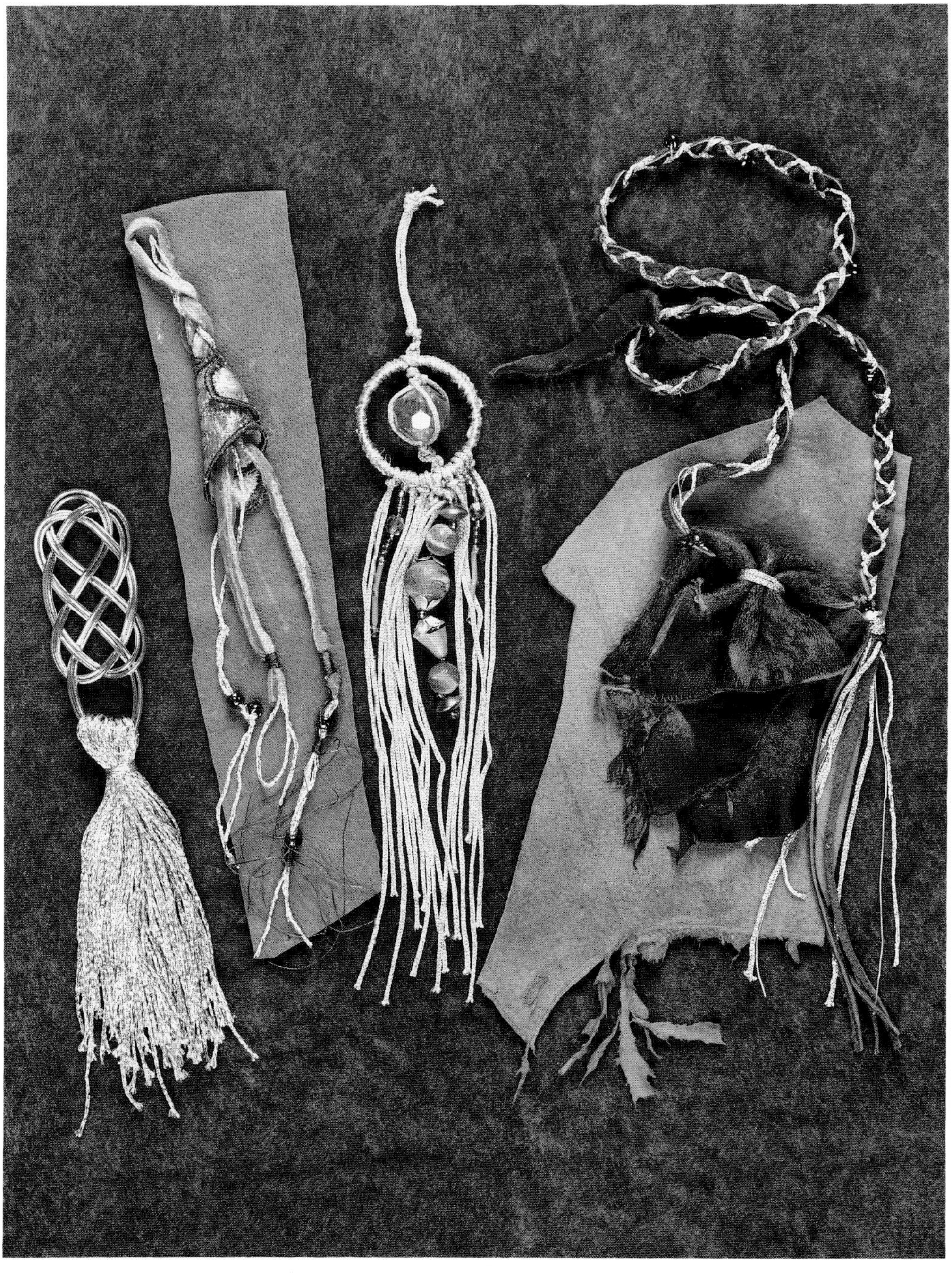

Carrick mat knot, rolled head & lark's head knot. Left – a decorative Carrick mat knot holds this rich little tassel made from metallic yarn. Second from left – a head made by the rolled fabric overskirt method holds a skirt of rouleaux cords. Second from right – the head is a detached buttonhole stitched soft plastic ring enclosing a large bead. The skirt is metallic cording tied with lark's head knots and some strings of beads. Right – suede purse with a three strand plaited braid handle.

Chapter 5

Knots

Knots can be functional in that they tie and secure in a myriad of different ways and span many crafts such as ropecraft, macrame and weaving - as well as embroidery and crocheting.

Decorative knots are appreciated for their own particular beauty to enhance all forms of trimmings.

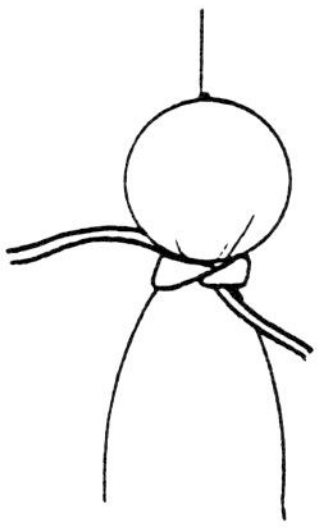
Fig. 14a

Functional Knots

Collecting knot

A collecting knot is a flat or reef knot used to unite two or more threads (as in macrame).

Double tie and wrap

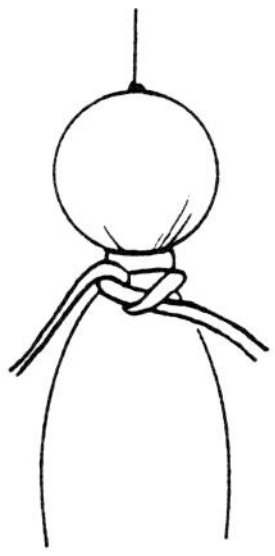
Fig. 14b

This process was discovered by the author as an alternative to wrapping short distances such as tassel necks. It was found to be a much easier way of controlling the two ends of the wrapping yarn.

1. Cut a piece of yarn approximately 46 cm (18 in) long and tie it around the neck of the tassel in an overhand knot. Figure 14a.
2. Turn the tassel to the back and tie a second overhand knot. This holds the threads temporarily in place. Figure 14b.
3. Wrap both tail ends, one at a time, in the opposite direction to each other around the bunch of tassel yarns for the desired width of wrapping.
4. Thread the yarn ends one at a time into a tapestry needle and bury them into the skirt of the tassel. Figure 14c.

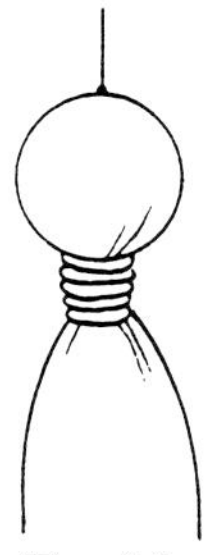
Fig. 14c

Granny knot

This commonly used knot is made when two overhand knots are tied together. It is not as secure as a reef knot because the knots slip. It is useful however to tie a granny knot before finishing off with the second procedure of the reef knot as it temporarily holds bunches of threads in place.

Lark's head knot

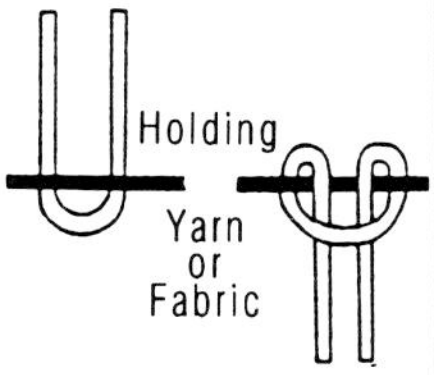

Fig. 15

This is a useful fringing knot also used in macrame and tatting.

1. Cut a length of yarn twice the size of the finished fringe and fold it in half.

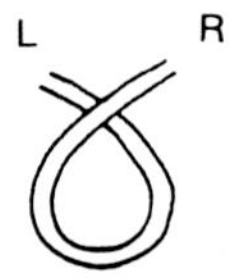

Fig. 16a

2. Place the fringing yarn with the loop downwards and behind the holding thread as in Figure 15.
3. Bring the ends down in front of the holding thread and through the loop created by the fringing yarn.
4. To secure, tighten both hanging ends equally.

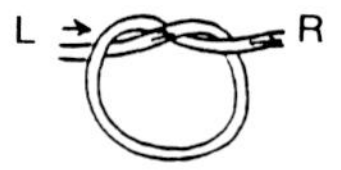

Fig. 16b

Overhand knot

This well known knot is commonly used as an initial 'stopper' procedure prior to more secure fastenings.

1. Refer to Figure 16 which shows a loop being formed by placing the right end over the left.
2. Pass the right hand end behind the loop, under and forward through the loop. Pull firmly.

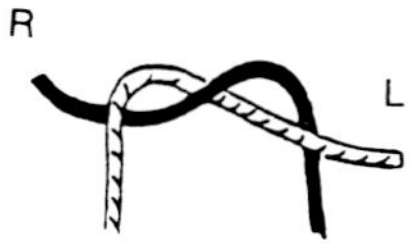

Fig. 17a

Reef knot, flat knot or square knot

This knot is a very secure way to finish off yarns. Refer to Figure 17a

1. Pass left end over right, under and forward.
2. Bring ends up and pass right behind left, Figure 17b, and bring left behind, under and over right – Figure 17c.
3. Pull ends to tighten.

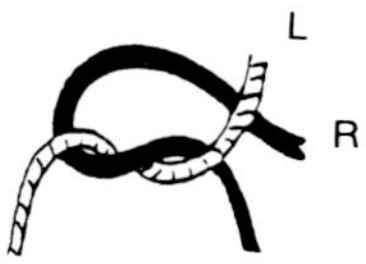

Fig. 17b

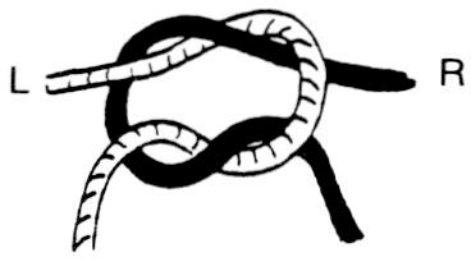

Fig. 17c

Wrap knot

1. The end of the wrapping yarn, shown as A in Figure 18 is placed over the yarns to be wrapped.
2. A loop is formed at B.
3. The long end of the yarn, shown as C is wrapped around the bunch of yarn for the desired distance and the end C is taken through loop B.
4. Pull end A firmly so that the tail C is hidden behind the wrapped threads.
5. Trim excess ends.

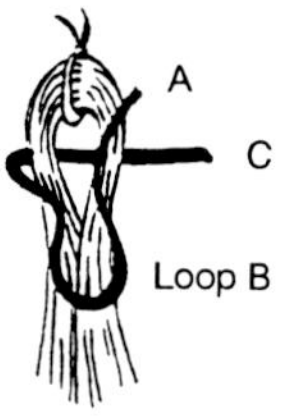

Fig. 18a

Another method is to lay a v-shaped piece of fine wire or cord along the part to be wrapped, then follow 4 and 5 above.

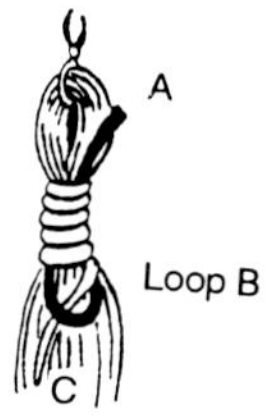

Fig. 18b

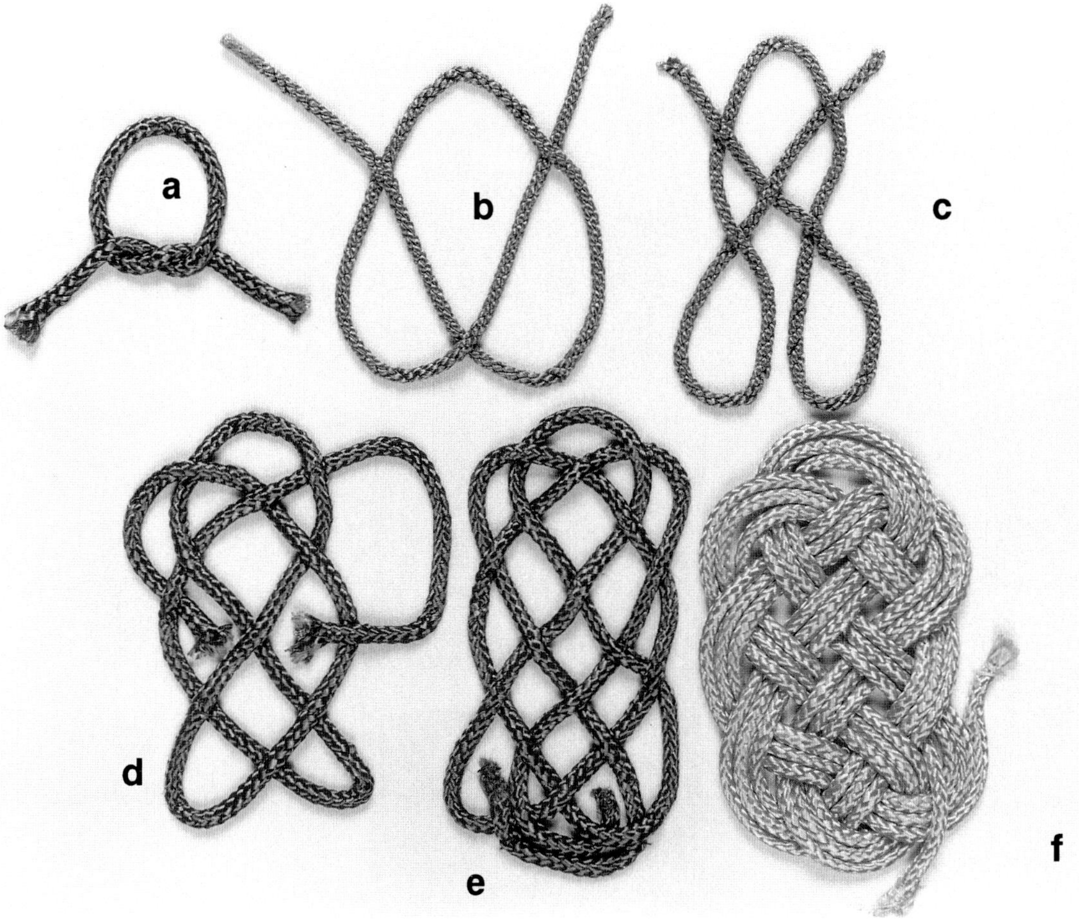

Carrick mat instructions

Decorative knots

Carrick mat knot – Photos page 68 and above

The above photo shows the workings of this knot which is best worked on a soft pinboard. Allow sufficient yarn to work this procedure, approximately 4-5 metres (5-6 yds)

1. Make an overhand knot as shown in a.
2. Extend the two loops down as shown in b.
3. Twist both the loops over to the right as in c.
4. Cross the right hand loop over the left hand loop.
5. Weave the ends as shown in d and e to complete the first round of the knot.
6. To make two, three or more strands to this knot weave the lead under and over in the same way as the first round as in f.

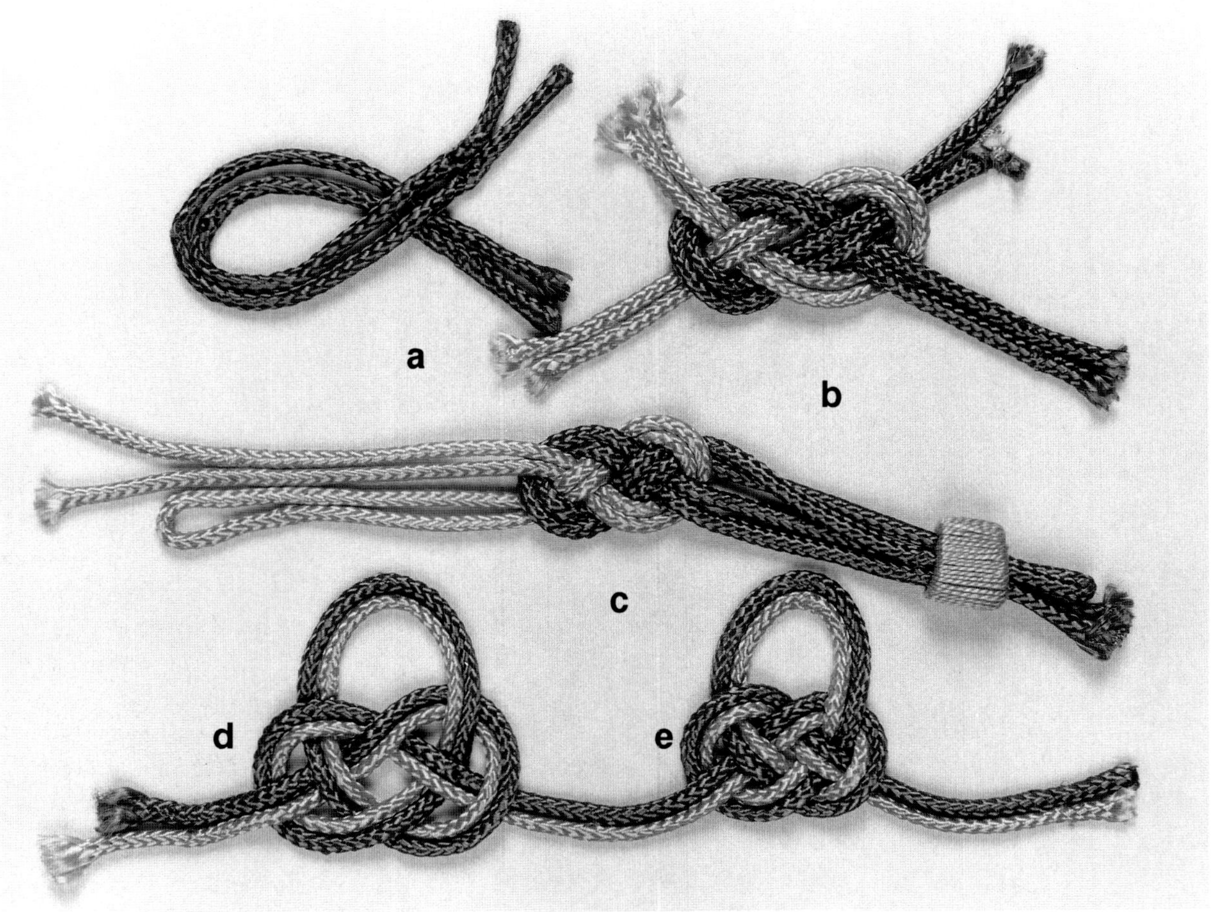

Josephine knot and Josephine knot looped – top and centre show the method of making a Josephine knot. Below this is the Josephine knot, looped.

Josephine knot

Photo above a, b and c clearly show the way to work this knot. Two or more groups of yarn, each laid side by side and kept flat, make a more attractive knot than one yarn.

One yarn made into a knot by this method and the ends stitched in place creates a ball button as described in 'frogging' in Chapter 3.

Josephine knot, looped

Above photo d and e clearly show the way to work this knot. As can be seen from this photo more than one knot may be tied on the one length of yarn.

Loop knot – Photo page 73

Photo page 73 clearly shows the steps required to make this decorative knot.

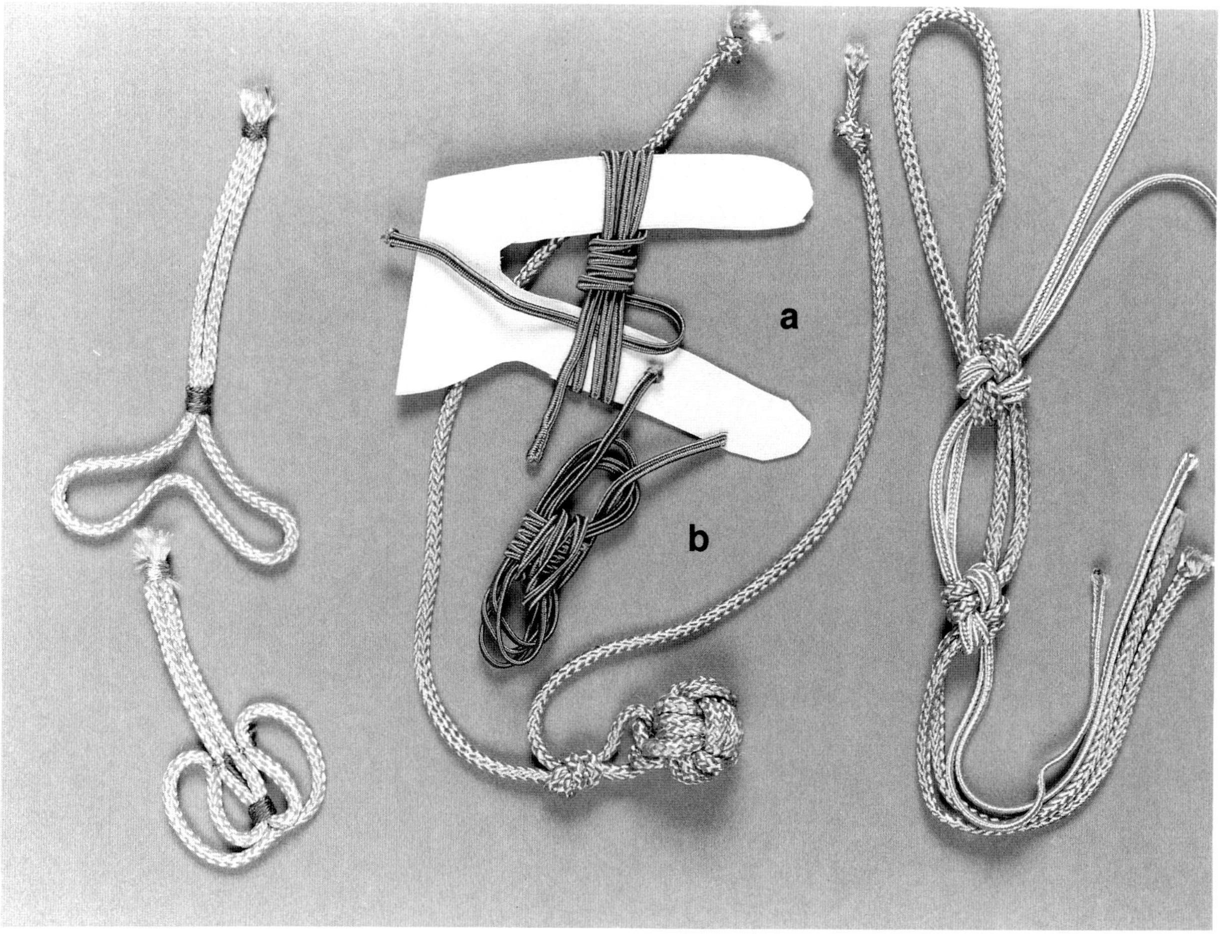

Left – loop knot   Centre – monkey's fist knot   Right – two decorative square knots

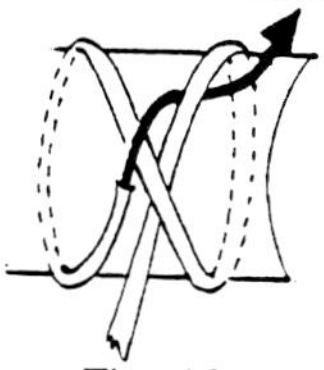

Fig. 19a

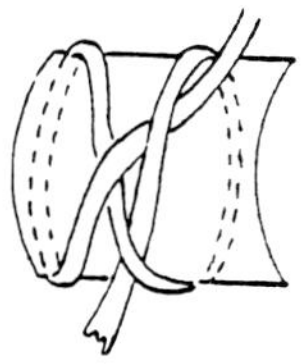

Fig. 19b

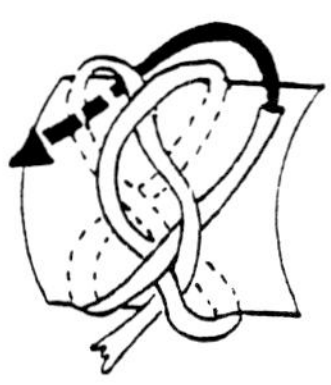

Fig. 19c

Monkey's fist knot – Photo above

This knot, when pulled tight, makes an ideal button or is used to make a plaited tassel as described in Chapter 1.

1. The knot is commenced by winding a length of yarn four times around the first two fingers of the left hand, and then four times over previous coils, between the fingers as in a.
2. Remove the fingers and wind four more coils into the previous ones as in b.
3. Tighten into a small ball by pulling each loop through the knot.

Turk's head knot, cylindrical – Figure 19

Allow sufficient yarn to complete this project, approximately 3-4 m (4-5 yds) of cord for a cylinder approximately 4 cm (1.5 in) in diameter. It is best to start with thick round cording rather than flat cording or narrow yarn.

The knot is usually worked around a cylinder or dowel stick to suit the size required.

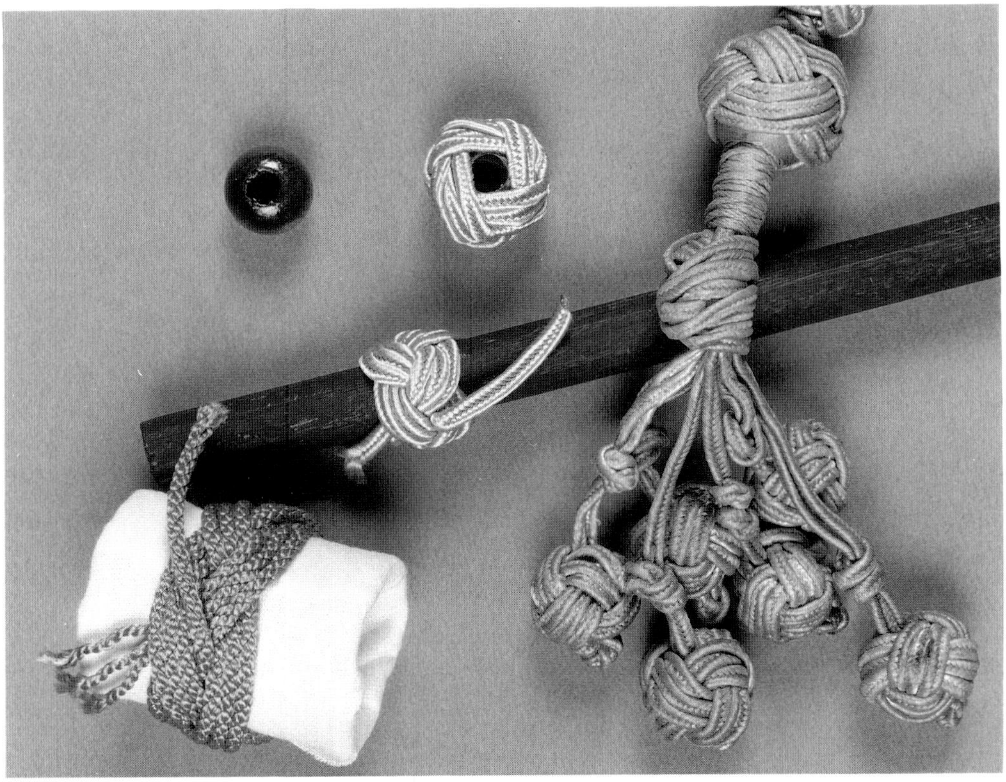

Bottom left shows a completed Turk's head knot, cylindrical ready for the end to be stitched in place and trimmed. Top – the finished knot is slipped onto a wooden bead. Right – plaited tassel.

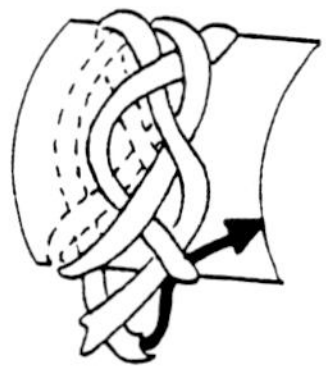

Fig. 19d

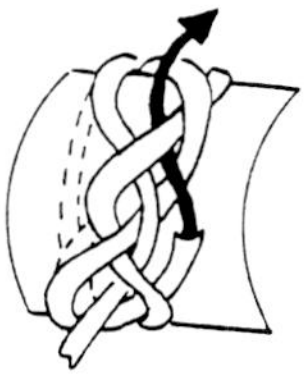

Fig. 19e

1. Figure 19a shows the first wrap having parallel lines at the back of the cylinder and crossing over at the front.
2. Take the lead in the direction of the arrow. A large knitter's needle assists in passing the lead under and over the cording.
3. Take the left hand loop at the top of the cylinder and cross it over the right hand loop at the top as indicated by the arrows at the top of Figure 19b.
4. Take the lead from right to left as indicated by the arrow in Figure 19c.
5. One opening will be found to remain, Figure 19d, into which the lead is passed from left to right. On viewing the work from the other side of the working end the lead will be found to have returned to the point of origin, lying alongside the other end and leading in the same direction. The knot is completed.

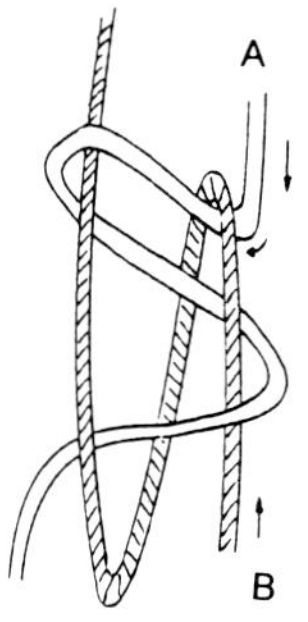

Fig. 20a

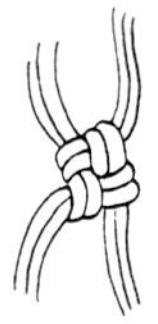

Fig. 20b

6. The lead is now passed over and under around the knot for a second, third or fourth time, following exactly the course of the first turns. Figure 19e.
7. The ends are stitched under the cord at the point of origin and then trimmed. Refer to Photo page 74 for examples.

Square decorative knot.

Plate XIII and scarf ring in Plate IX, Photo page 74 and Figure 20.

Figure 20a shows how to make this lovely decorative knot which can be used on cords, curtain tie backs and anywhere a decorative knot is required.

It is usually worked with two lots of thick double cords and looping is commenced in the middle of the cords.

The diagram in Figure 20a shows the cord as a single line but it is best worked with two doubled lengths of cord, A and B.

1. Make loop A as shown.
2. Interlace loop B as shown.

Carefully tighten the knot so that it resembles Figure 20b.

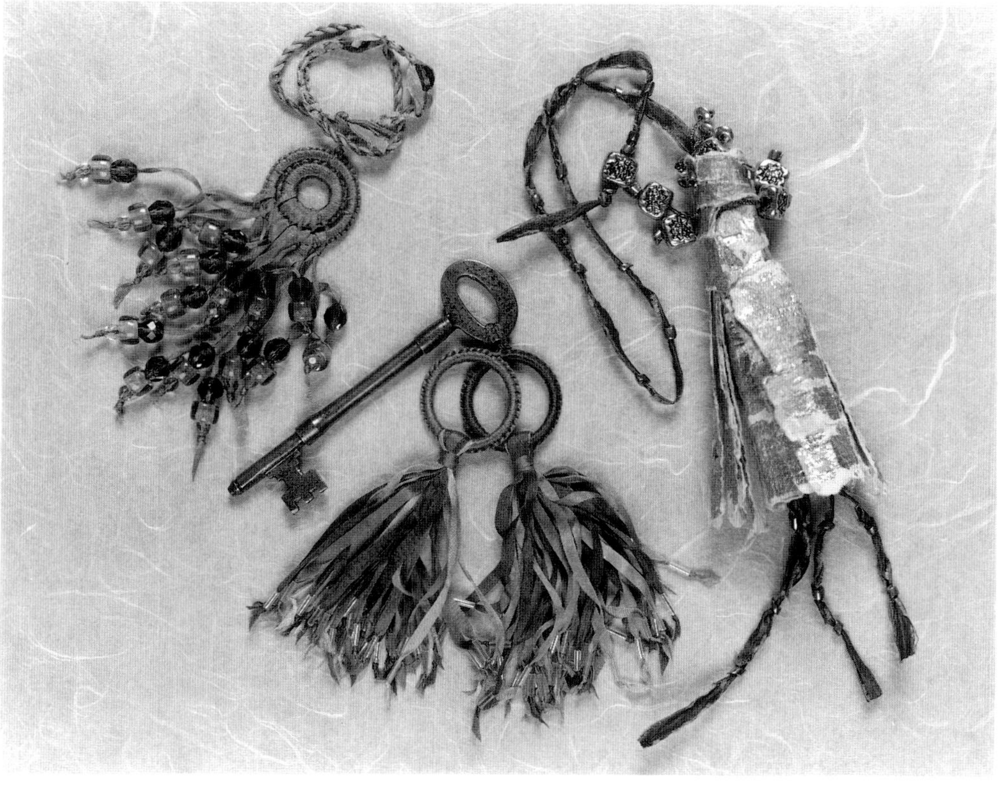

Unique tassels. Joan Jeffries' tassel is made from silk ribbon, beads and detached buttonholed metal rings. Centre - Alison Snepp's key tassel is made from silk ribbon, bugle beads and metal rings covered with alternating detached buttonhole stitch. Patricia Langford's gilded hand made paper tassel incorporates metal beads and a cord made from torn fabric.

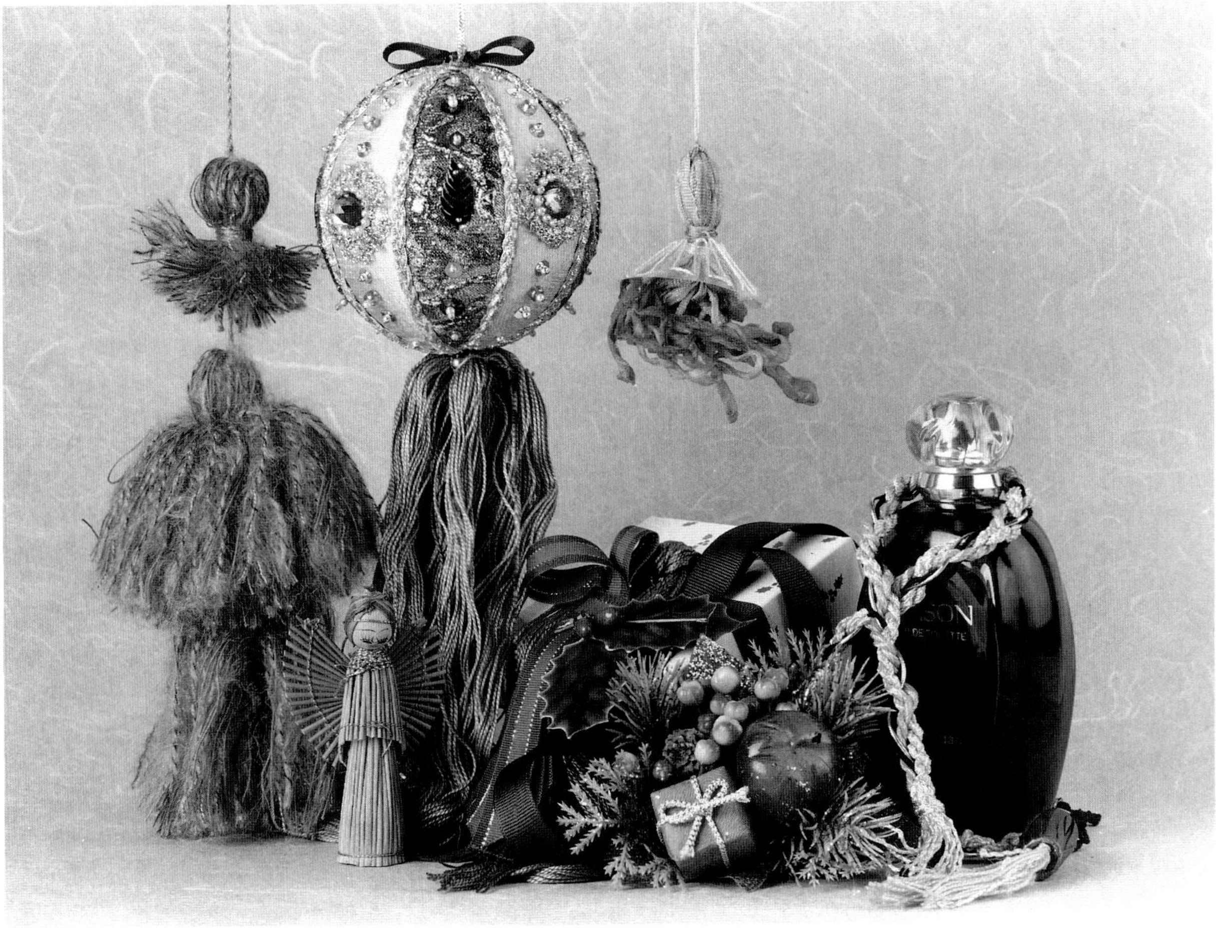

Gift wrapped for Christmas. Top row Left - a fluffy green multi-layered mohair tassel. Middle - a polystyrene ball has been decorated by Robyn Hayden in rich silk and brocade fabrics, gold lace, beads and sequins and metres of metallic three strand plaited braid cord. Right - a plastic collar stitched with metallic crochet yarn covers a tassel made of space dyed knitting ribbon. The unique 'flying' effect is created by first dipping the ribbon tassel in fabric stiffener then attaching the collar. Bottom row Left - a store bought Christmas tree angel has all the makings of a tassel. Centre - gift box tied with tasselled ribbons. Right - perfume bottle decorated with rich braided cords and a tassel on the end which is finished off with a length of wrapped plastic tubing.

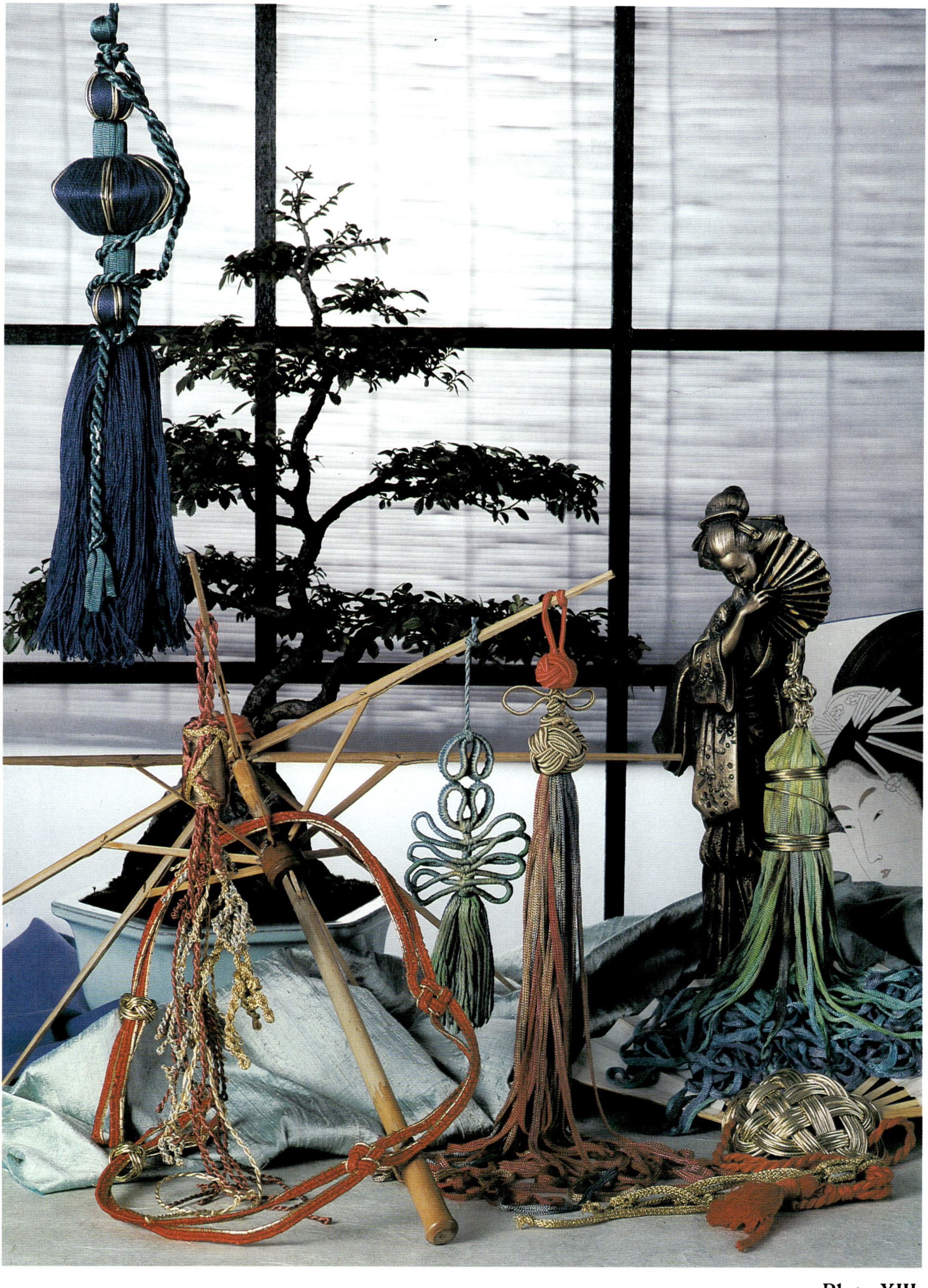

Plate XIII

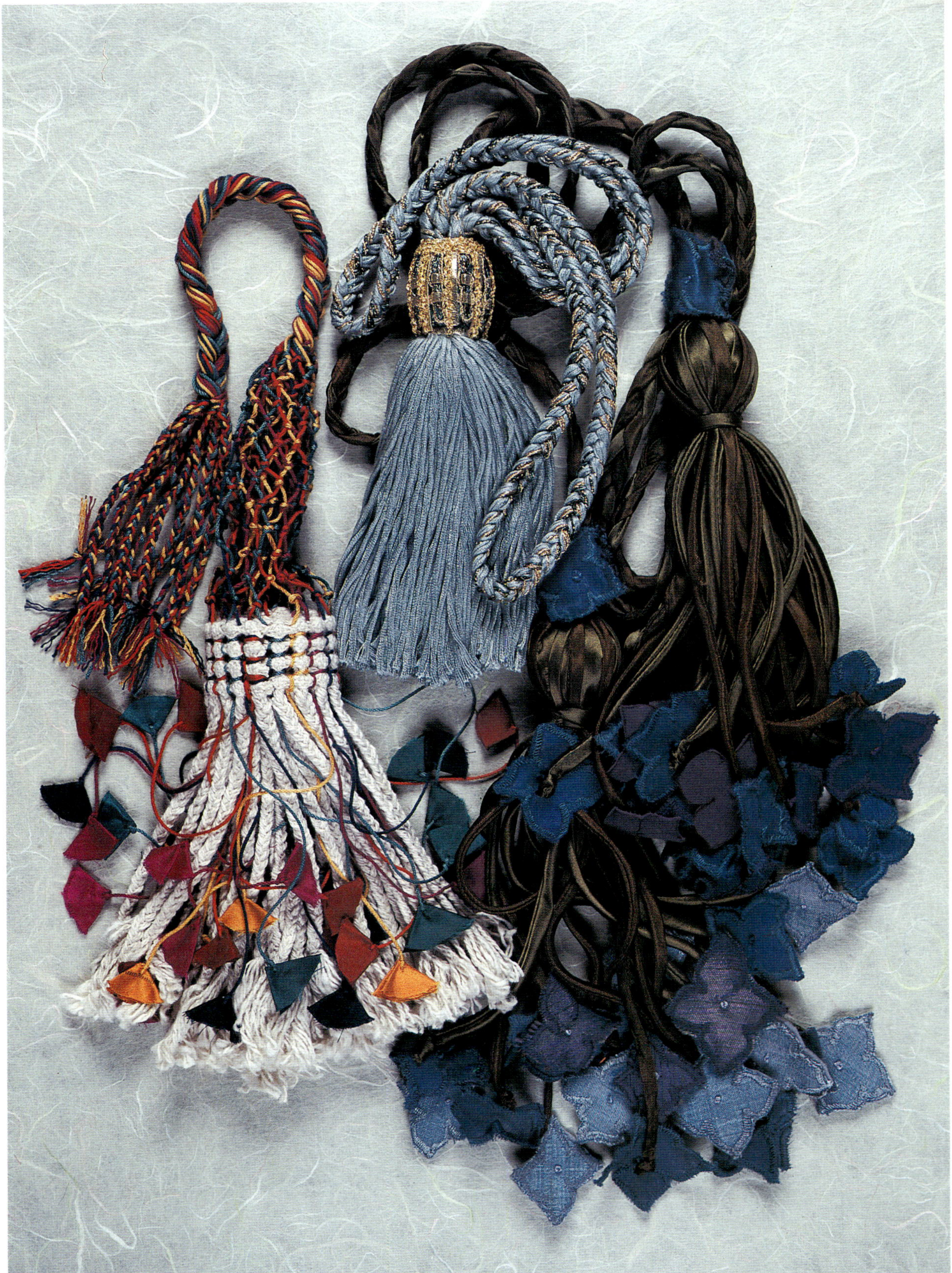

Plate XIV

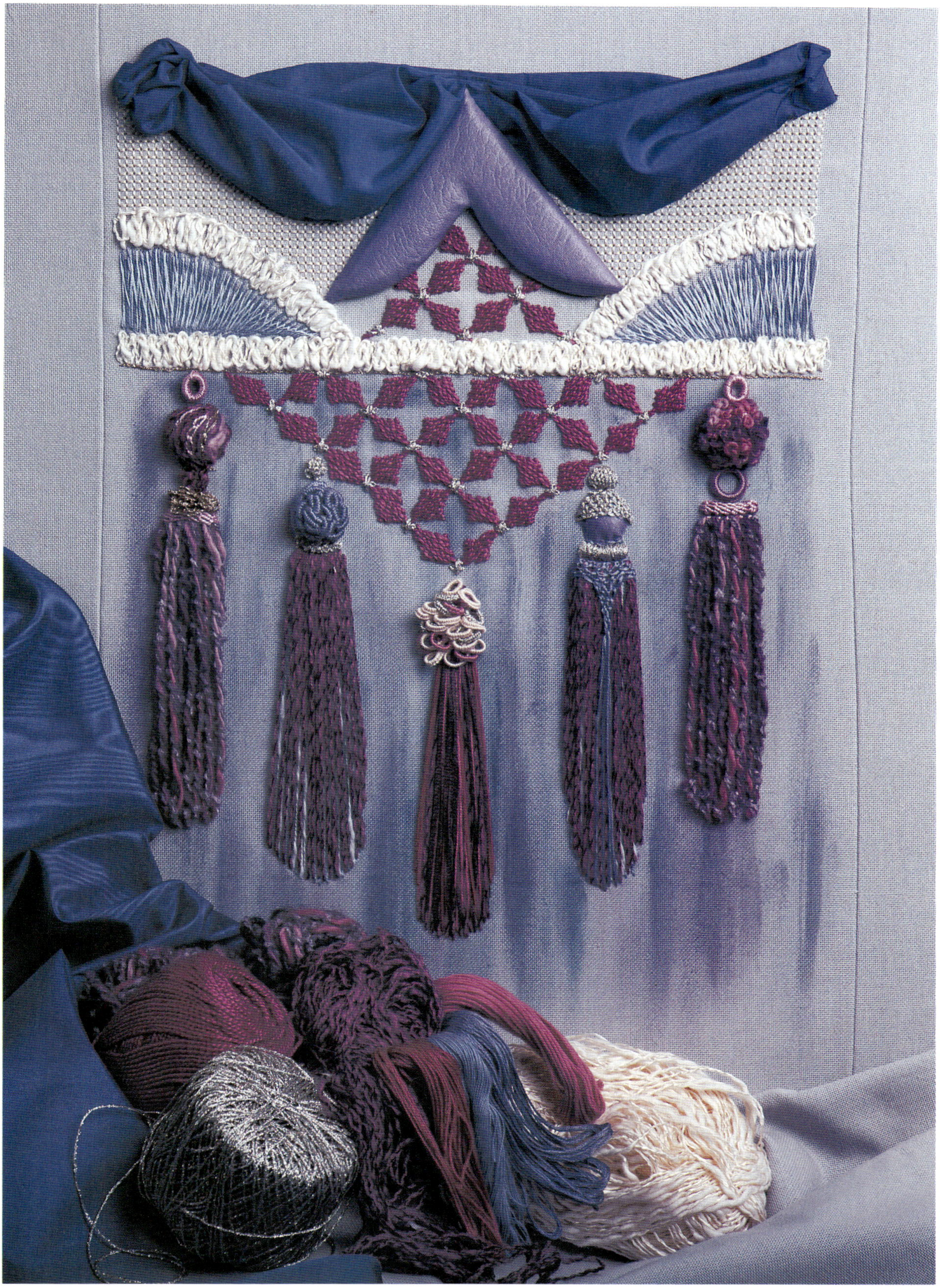

Plate XV

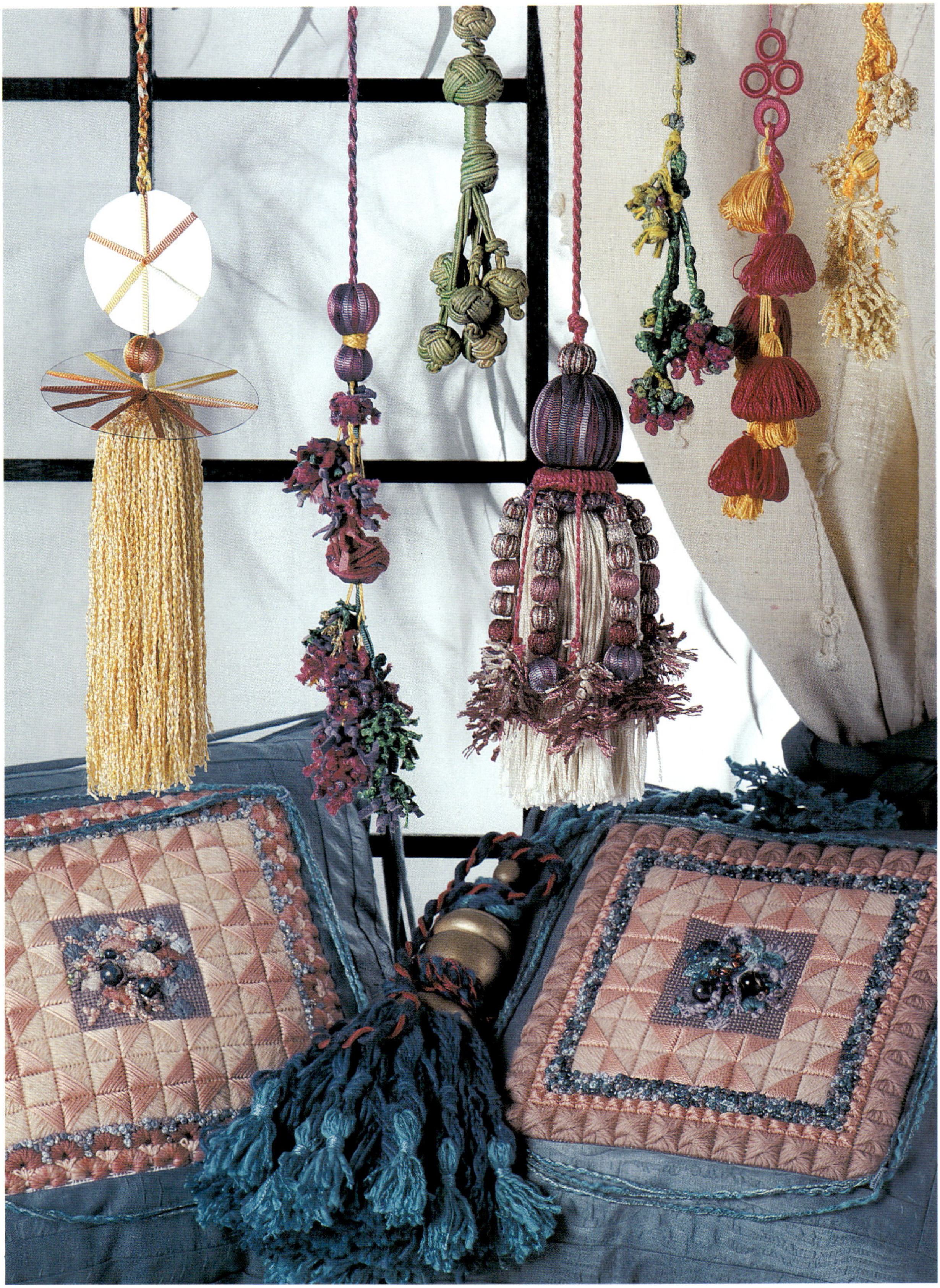

Plate XVI

Plate XIII Oriental

Top left - vertically wrapped wooden beads, plastic tubing and a sculptured polystyrene ball are the foundations used to make this elegant tassel. Bottom row - left to right. Left - a plastic bottle top was covered in metallic leather and twisted cords. Ribbon and metallic crochet yarn were randomly twisted on the sewing machine to create the skirt. Behind the tassel and threaded through the umbrella frame is a curtain tieback made of machine made Russia type braid. Cylindrical Turk's head knots are placed at the end of the loops while two decorative square knots are tied between them. 2nd from left - loop knots made with detached buttonholed soft plastic milk bottle top rings joined to a wrapped and looped tassel. 2nd from right - dyed ribbon forms the skirt topped with two cylindrical Turk's head knots over wooden beads. The Turk's head knots and the loops of the holding cord are made in purchased Russia braid. Right - hanging from a Japanese statuette is a tassel secured by horizontal gold wrapped cord over a pierced plastic pill bottle. The holding cord features a cylindrical Turk's head knot. In front of this tassel is a Carrick mat knot made of gold cord which could be used as a hairpiece or belt buckle.

Plate XIV - Original Tassels

Left - Karma Victoria Bains' original tassel is made from a cotton dishcloth the centre of which was worked with four sided stitch. Below this horizontal weft threads were withdrawn and plaited and silk fabric pieces attached with coloured yarn. The coloured yarn is knotted and plaited at the top of the tassel. Centre - Janice Rawlinson has made a rich tassel from cotton knitting yarn held by a cord of three strand braid incorporating metal thread. The head has been stitched with leather and metal thread. Right - Heather Joynes' original tassels made of satin rouleaux cords decorate a belt at each end. Machine made fabric hydrangea flowers are attached to the heads and skirts.

Plate XV - Draped Window - Stitch Sampler

This page is a stitch sampler showing in the top one third - four sided stitch; curves of rosette chain band in bubbly yarn and three rows of Cretan stitch worked on top of each other. A line of braid stitch in bubbly yarn divides the top section from the tassels which hang from a lattice pattern of stem stitch with two chain stitches crossed on top of each other at the intersections. Tassels from left to right. Left - top, down - detached buttonhole plastic tubing; lines of chain stitch over a foundation of half a wooden bead covered with fabric; neck of Ghiordes knot and raised stem band stitch; straight stitch skirt. Second from left - top, down - a cluster of French knots, bullion knots worked over a foundation of half a wooden bead covered with fabric; neck of French knots; straight stitch skirt. Middle - head of soft detached buttonhole rings worked around a pencil; straight stitch skirt. Second from right - top, down - padded raised stem band; head is multi layers of felt padding covered with leather with detached buttonhole worked to half way down the head. Neck is vertical wrapping; straight stitch skirt with an overskirt of detached buttonhole stitch. Right - top, down - detached buttonhole plastic ring; French knots over a foundation of half a wooden bead covered in fabric; detached buttonhole plastic ring; neck of raised stem band; straight stitch skirt.

Plate XVI - Soft Furnishings

Two canvas work (needlepoint) embroidered cushions are laced with rouleaux cords through a loop at each corner. Machine made cords using knitting yarn and metallic machine yarn decorate the edges of the needlepoint threaded through soft detached buttonhole loops which are stitched to the cushion cover. Between the two cushions nestles a large tassel made from a gold painted wooden curtain rod end. An overskirt is made of tassels with a collar of Ghiordes knot stitch. Row of tassels, top Left - circles of firm plastic and a wooden bead have been wrapped with space dyed knitting ribbon to achieve this space age tassel. Second from left - knotted ball tassel made of space dyed yarn and knitting ribbon. Beads on the holding cord have been wrapped, the lowest one covered with a cylindrical Turk's head knot. Third from left - this plaited tassel was first made in one pale shade of purchased Russia braid. It was then painted with fabric paint including metallic gold. Fourth from left - this tassel features many foundations. The head is a painted polystyrene ball pierced to form a hole down the centre and wrapped with space dyed knitting yarn. A collar made from a detached buttonholed plastic curtain ring holds strings of wrapped beads. Alternating between these strings are knotted ball tassels. Third from right - double knotted ball tassels made from space dyed knitting ribbon. Second from right - detached buttonholed plastic rings and washer hold a string of fuchsia tassels. Right - a knotted ball tassel made from cording.

Chapter 6

Stitches and Embroidered Knots

These stitches and embroidered knots have been chosen for both functional and decorative reasons. Most of the stitches are shown on Plate XV.

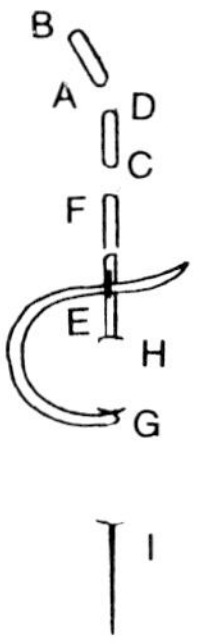

Fig. 21

Back stitch – Figure 21

Bring the needle and yarn out at A, down into B and out at C. Repeat. The basic movement of this stitch is one step back and two steps forward and is usually worked from right to left. The reverse side automatically forms stem stitch.

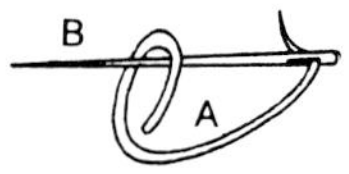

Fig. 22a

Braid stitch

This lovely textured stitch makes an attractive trimming to edges and as a braid stitched directly onto fabric, ribbon or tassel.

1. Bring needle and yarn out at A. Pick up a loop of yarn with the needle as in Figure 22a.
2. Make sure that you form the loop as shown in Figure 22b.
3. Repeat this process as in Figure 22c.

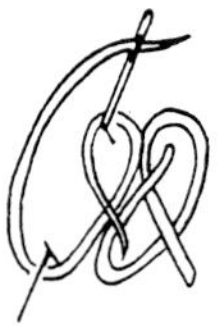

Fig. 22b

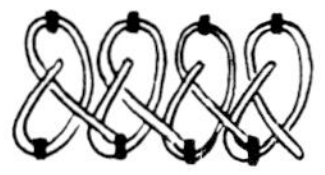

Fig. 22c

This stitch is fairly loose and works best closely packed and not too deep. If you wish to make a wider, broader braid take small back stitches through the loops on both sides of the braid. These could be worked in a matching or contrasting yarn as a feature.

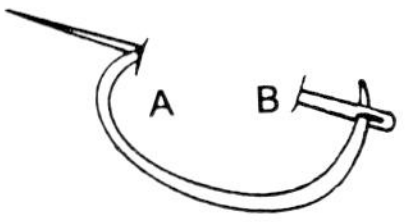

Fig. 23a

Bullion knot stitch

1. Bring needle and yarn out at A, down into B and out at A. Don't pull the yarn through yet. Refer Figure 23a.

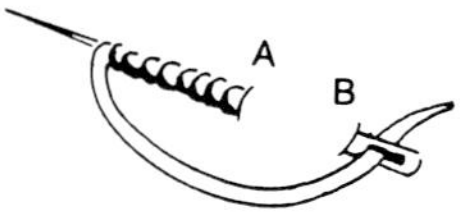

Fig. 23b

2. Loop the yarn round and round the needle six to ten or more times at A. Refer Figure 23b. It is best to wind the thread around the thicker part of the needle, not too tight or too loose. A straw needle facilitates this stitch.
3. With the left thumb and index finger hold the wound loops and needle firmly and with the right hand pull the needle gently through the coils, alternately holding and releasing the wound thread to allow the needle to pull through.
4. To distribute the coils of the knot evenly, gently pull the thread while the left thumbnail holds the coils - refer Figure 23c.

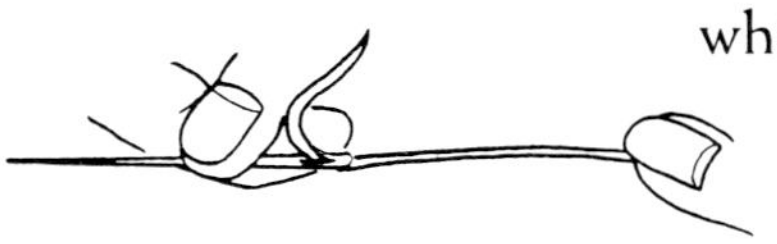
Fig. 23c

Buttonhole stitch – Figure 24

1. Bring needle and yarn out of fabric at A.
2. Insert needle through B-C.

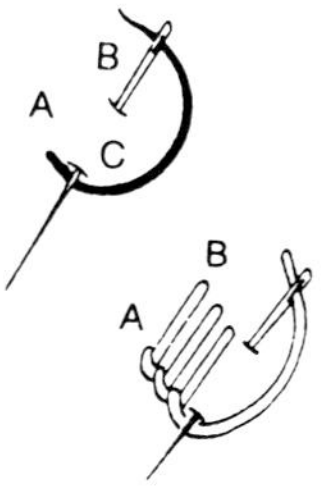

Fig. 24

3. Loop yarn under the needle and pull needle and yarn through the fabric.
4. Repeat.

This stitch worked closely packed forms a secure edging.

Chain stitch – Figure 25a

1. Bring needle and yarn out at A.
2. Insert needle through A-B.
3. Loop yarn under needle and pull needle and yarn through the fabric.
4. Repeat 2 and 3 above to form a line.

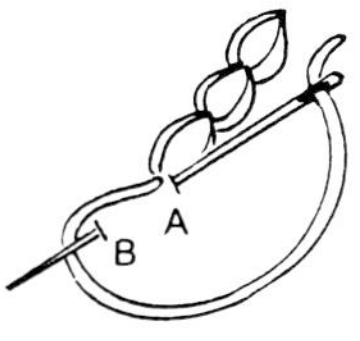

Fig. 25a

Chain stitch, detached

1. Following steps 1 to 3 for chain stitch take needle and yarn down into C. This secures the loop and forms a detached chain. Refer Figure 25b.

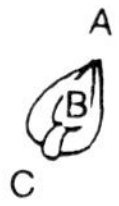

Fig. 25b

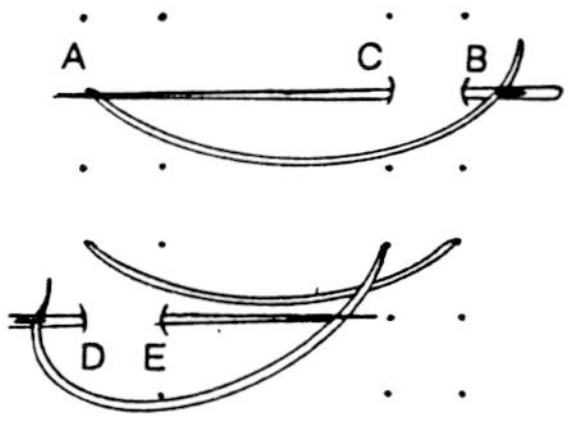

Fig. 26a

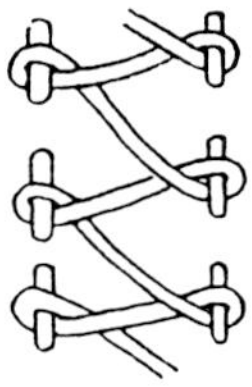
Fig. 26b

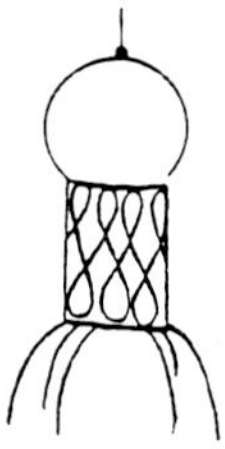
Fig. 26c

Cretan stitch

Bring needle and yarn out at A, down through B-C, forming a loop under the needle and under B-C as in Figure 26a.
Figure 26b shows Cretan stitch being laced between two lines of back stitch.
Figure 26c shows Cretan stitch worked on the wrapped neck of a tassel.

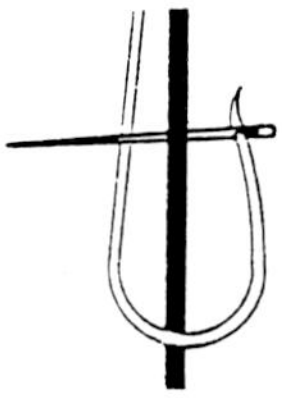
Fig. 27a

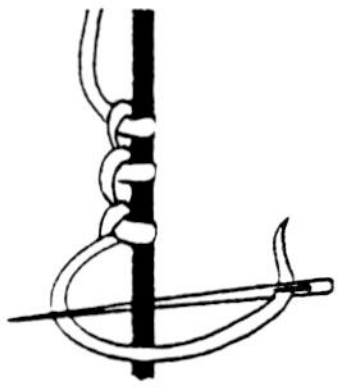
Fig. 27b

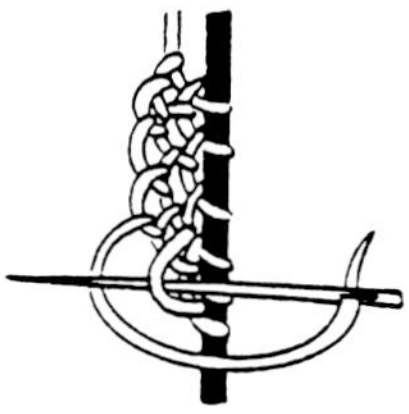
Fig. 27c

Detached buttonhole stitch

The same movement as buttonhole stitch is used for detached buttonhole except that it is not worked completely on fabric but around a core or holding thread or upon itself. Detached buttonhole may be attached to fabric by an initial row of back stitches.

Figure 27c shows subsequent rows of detached buttonhole worked onto the previous row of detached buttonhole stitches. This forms a needlewoven cloth which may be worked loosely for open lace or with firm tension to create a closely woven fabric.

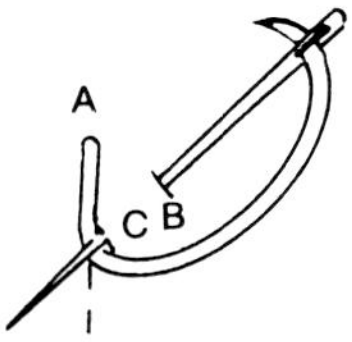

Fig. 28a

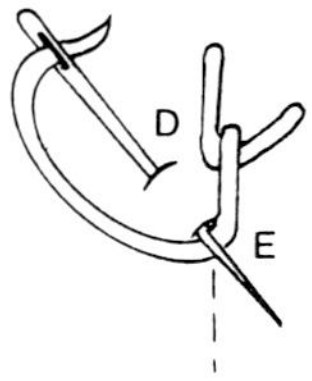

Fig. 28b

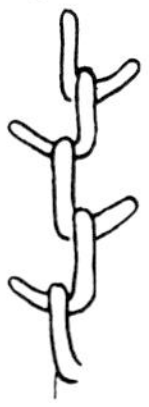

Fig. 28c

Feather stitch

This stitch may be used to decorate tassels and braids. It can be worked in any width, closely packed or openly spaced. The beauty of this stitch is that two or more rows may be worked one on top of the other in different weights of yarn to create a very attractive braid trimming.

1. Bring needle and yarn out at A in Figure 28a. Form a loop with the yarn and take needle and yarn through B-C.
2. Repeat this process but instead of inserting the needle to the right of the line A-C, work on the left through D-E as shown in Figures 28b and c.

Four sided stitch

This pulled thread stitch is worked on linen fabric to achieve a lacy effect created by pulling each stitch firmly. It is also useful as a finishing edge combined with frayed fabric edges as in bookmarks, mats and fabric tassel edges. Suitable threads are coton perle No. 5 and 8 equivalents or crocheting or knitting yarns, depending on the thickness of the fabric and the desired effect.

Fig. 29

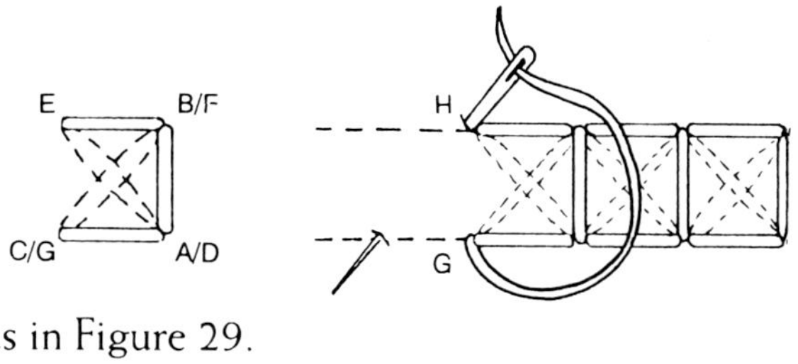

1. Bring needle out at A as in Figure 29.
2. Take needle and yarn down into B and out at C, pull stitch firmly to create a hole in the fabric.
3. Take needle and yarn down into D and out at E, pulling stitch firmly again.
4. Take needle and yarn down into F and out at G, pulling stitch firmly.

It will be noted that a diagonal cross forms at the back of the work as shown by the dotted lines.

5. Repeat 1, 2 and 3 for the desired length.

French knot stitch

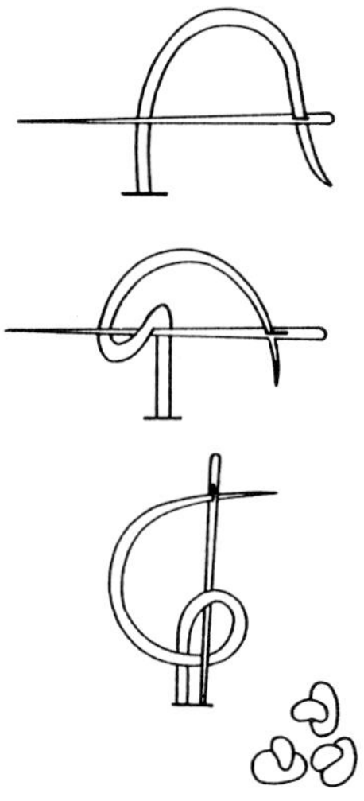

Fig. 30

1. Bring needle and yarn out at A.
2. Hold yarn with the thumb and rest the needle on top of the yarn.
3. Twist the yarn around the needle once as shown in Figure 30.
4. Twist the needle sideways and towards you and insert it into the fabric at B. Pull yarn through.
5. While pulling the yarn through hold it well clear of the knot until all the thread has been pulled to the back. This will prevent tangles and allow better tension control.

Ghiordes knot stitch – Figure 31 and Photo page 42

Traditionally a canvas work stitch, Ghiordes knot is ideal for making loops to decorate tassel moulds. Mark the area to be worked in pencil on the canvas - an average measurement is 12 mm (.5 in) wide by the length around the neck of the tassel. Machine stitch close zigzag stitch or apply fray check around the marked area. Place canvas in a hoop or frame and work the Ghiordes knot stitch from the bottom row upwards. When using thick cord as yarn a larger needle and open mesh canvas need to be used. When the stitching is complete cut around the marked shape and stitch in place onto tassel.

1. Bring needle and yarn out at A, down into B and out at C.
2. Create a free flowing loop between C and D coming out at A.
3. Repeat this procedure working the stitches in horizontal rows from the bottom row upwards. The size of the loop C-D may be controlled by holding it in place with the thumb or looping it around a knitting needle or pencil.

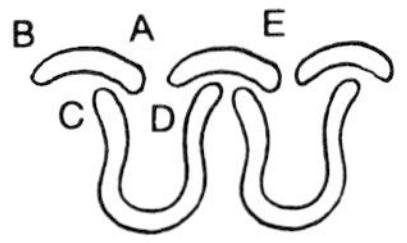

Fig. 31

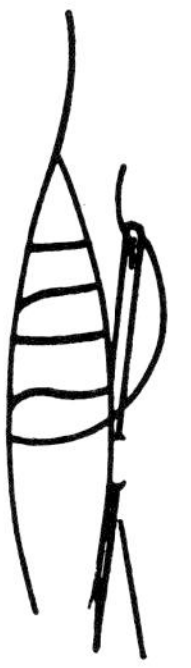
Fig. 32

Ladder stitch

Hand worked ladder stitching makes a concealed join of two seams.

1. Fold back the seam allowance for an open seam to be worked. It is important to note that each ladder stitch bridging the seam should form a right angle to the seam to which it is to be joined as shown in Figure 32 otherwise the stitches will show.
2. Bring the needle and sewing cotton out near the edge of the fabric, exactly on the fold of the fabric at A.
3. Take the needle across and down into the line of the seam to be joined. Make a small running stitch approximately 3 to 4 mm (up to .25 in) long on the seam line.
4. Bring the thread out and back across to the first seam line and take the next running stitch forward. Continue taking running stitches alternately in the joins for about 2.5 cm (1 in) then firmly pull the thread so that the join closes and the fabric rolls to conceal the stitches.
5. Continue working in this manner until the seam is completely joined.

Lock stitch

A lock stitch secures and finishes off the sewing or weaving yarn prior to cutting. It is simply two detached buttonhole stitches forming a knot.

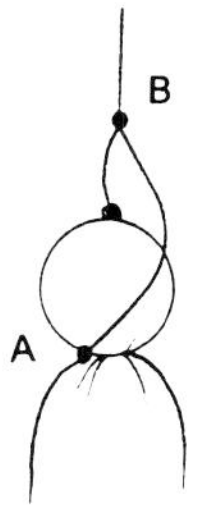

Fig. 33a

Needleweaving

Needleweaving, as the name suggests, is weaving with a needle and yarn as distinct from loom weaving.

Core or carrier - The stitches of needleweaving are formed over a core or carrier. This core may be created by withdrawing warp or weft threads from fabric leaving threads which can be used singly or in multiples as a core or carrier.

Alternately you may make your own core or carrying threads with the same yarn in the needle used for the weaving. An example of one is A-B in Figure 33a.

In tasselmaking the holding cord, neck and skirt offer ready made core or carrying threads.

You may make your own core on any part of the tassel and holding cord by securing a length of the yarn between any two points with lock stitches.

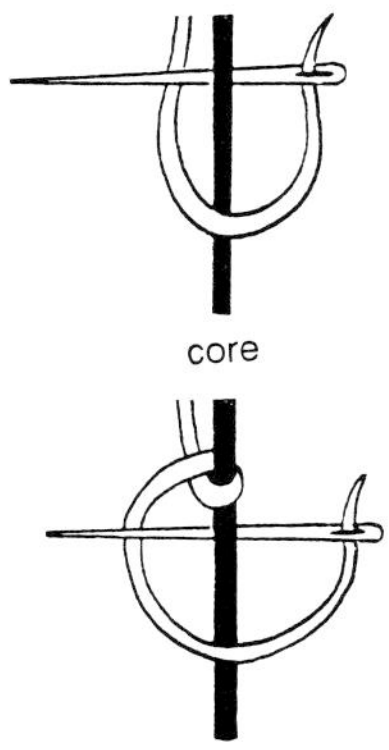

Fig. 33b

Detached buttonhole needleweaving

Make detached buttonhole stitches down the core or holding thread as shown in Figure 33b.

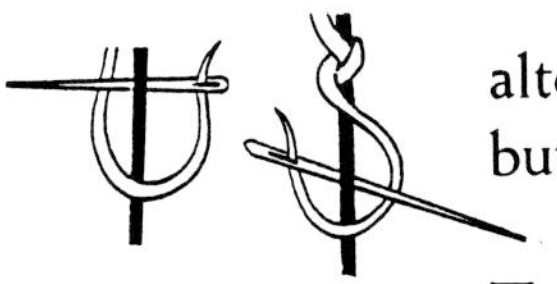

Fig. 33c

Alternating detached buttonhole needleweaving – Figure 33c

Make detached buttonhole stitches down the core or holding thread alternately from left to right. This makes a different effect from detached buttonhole needleweaving.

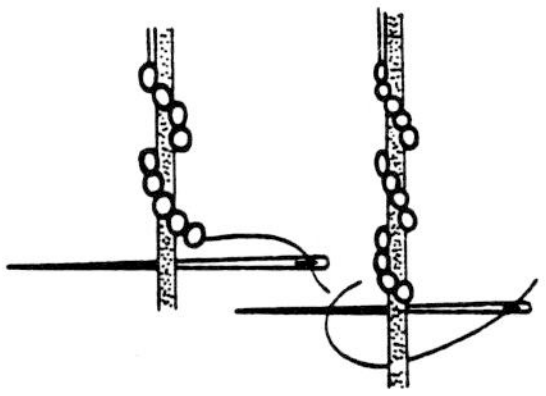

Fig. 34

Twisted detached buttonhole needleweaving

1. Make detached buttonhole stitches down the core or holding thread as shown in Figure 34.
2. After every five detached buttonhole stitches take the needle and weaving yarn behind and to the left hand side of the core. This will facilitate a twisted effect.
3. Repeat steps 1 and 2 above until the desired length is achieved.

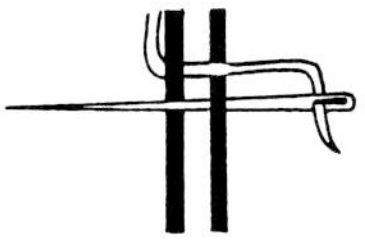

cores

Fig. 35a

Woven - plain weave needleweaving

Take needle and yarn under and over two or more core threads, weaving backwards and forwards as in Figures 35a and b.

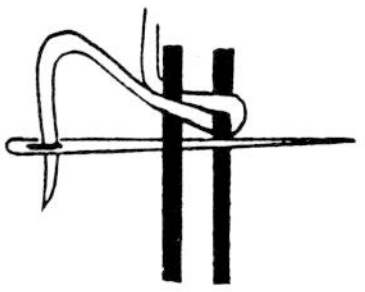

cores

Fig. 35b

Wrapping a core yarn – Figure 36

1. Take needle and yarn round and round core thread. This will result in a small cord.
2. To hold the weaving yarn in place while wrapping place your index finger under the core at the wrapping point.
3. Secure ends with lock stitch.

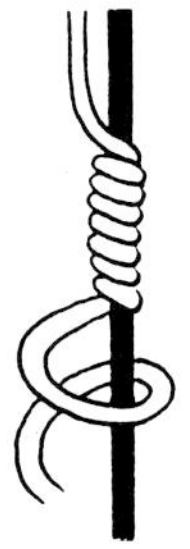

Fig. 36

Pekinese stitch

1. Work a line of back stitch.
2. With matching or contrasting thread make loops through the back stitch as shown in Figure 37.

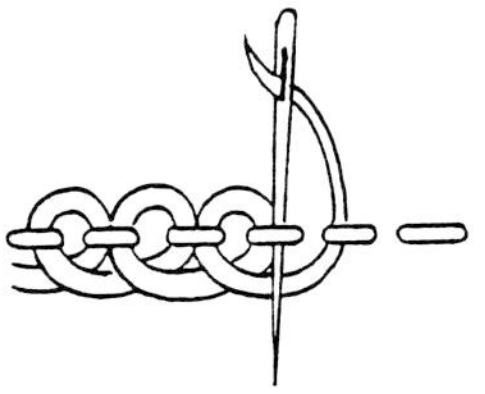

Fig. 37

Raised chain band stitch

1. First work a row of straight stitches to form foundation bars in matching or contrasting yarn onto which the raised chain band is to be worked. The bars are approximately 6 mm (.25 in) wide and the same distance apart although these measurements may be varied depending on the thickness of yarn used and the desired effect. When turning corners radiate the bars around the corners, as shown in Figure 38, the same as railway sleepers.

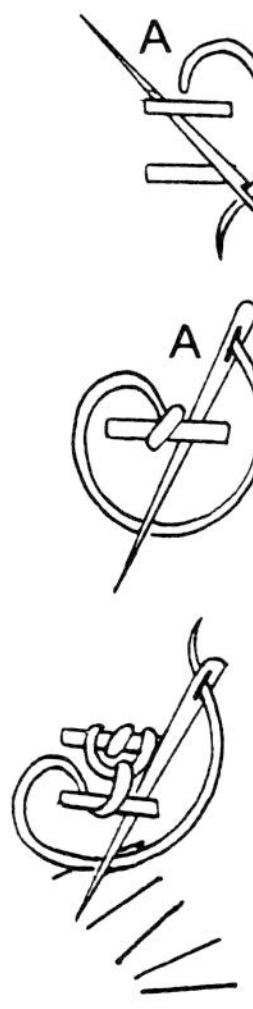

Fig. 38

2. To work the raised chain stitches bring needle and yarn out at A as shown in Figure 38.
3. Take the needle and yarn over the bar, under the bar and up to the left side of A. This can be described as the first of two movements.
4. Form a loop with the yarn and make a detached chain stitch as in Figure 38 - this is the second movement.

Repeat these two movements to create each raised chain taking note that the first movement of each stitch controls the tension of the previous stitch.

The needle and yarn don't pass through the fabric except to begin and finish off. If desired the bars may be made longer and two or more rows of raised chain stitches worked adjacent to each other on the bars.

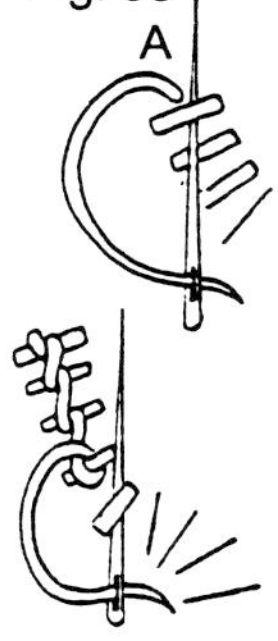

Fig. 39

Raised stem band stitch

1. Work foundation bars as described in 1 of raised chain band stitch above.
2. To form the raised stem stitches bring needle and yarn out at A. Work a row of stem stitches over the bars as in Figure 39.
3. If desired the foundation bars may be made wider and two or more rows of raised stem band worked adjacent to each other on the bars.

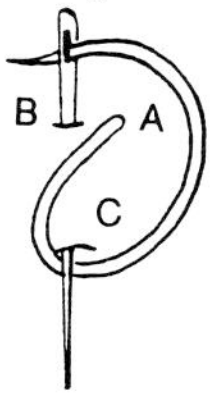

Fig. 40a

Rosette chain braid stitch

This stitch forms an attractive and decorative braid to trim clothing, furnishings and tassels.

1. Bring needle and thread out at A - refer Figure 40a.
2. Insert needle through fabric at B-C and loop yarn from A across to the left and under the needle. Pull yarn carefully through B-C to form a twisted chain.

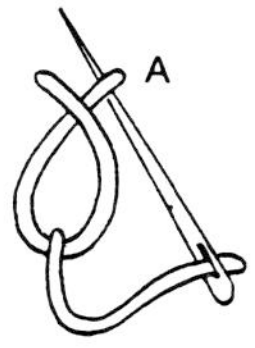

Fig. 40b

3. Take needle and yarn up and under yarn as shown in Figure 40b. leaving this loop fairly loose to form the rosette chain.

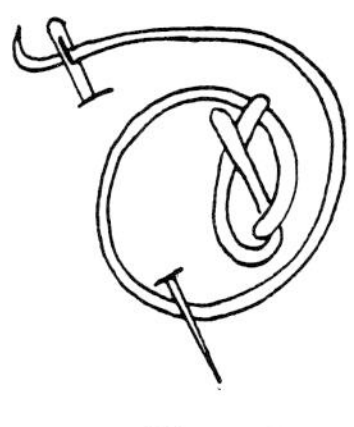
Fig. 40c

4. Repeat 2 and 3 above, next to the previous rosette chain and continue working for the desired length. Figure 40c.

As with braid stitch, rosette chain braid is fairly loose and works best closely packed and not too deep. However, if you wish to make a wider, broader braid take small back stitches through the loops on both sides of the braid to make it more secure.

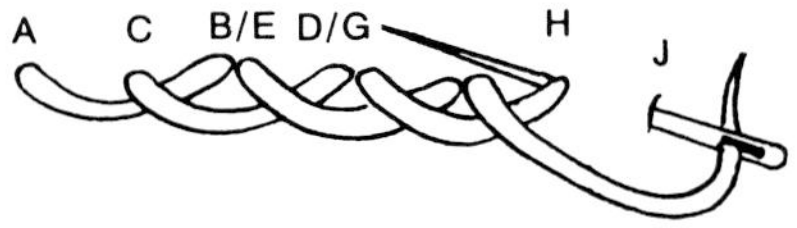

Fig. 41

Stem stitch – Figure 41

Bring the needle and yarn out at A, down into B and out at C, down into D, out at E, down into F, out at G, and so on. The basic movement of this stitch is two steps forward and one step back and it is usually worked from left to right.

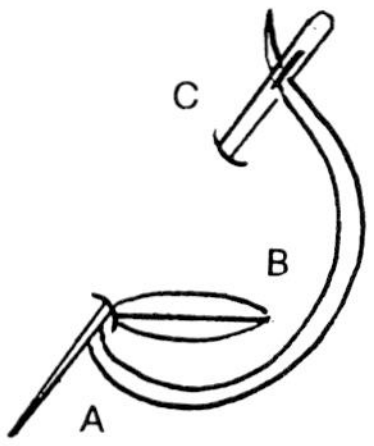

Fig. 42a

Three-sided stitch – Photo page 65

This is a pulled thread stitch usually worked over four threads.

1. As in Figure 42a come out at A and make two back stitches at A-B.
2. Make another back stitch, A-C coming out at A again, followed by a stitch forward and down into C and out at D – Figure 42b.
3. Make a back stitch A-D coming out at D, followed by a stitch back to A and out at E – Figure 42c.
4. Repeat steps 1 to 3.

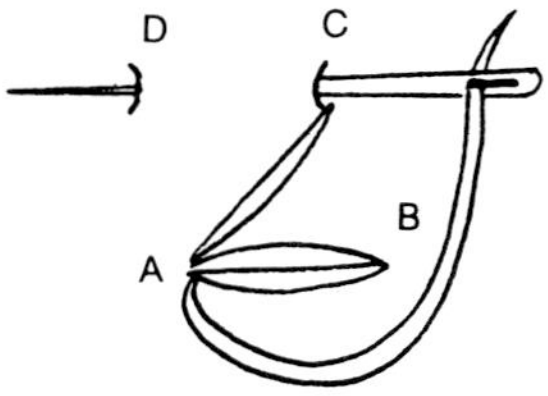

Fig. 42b

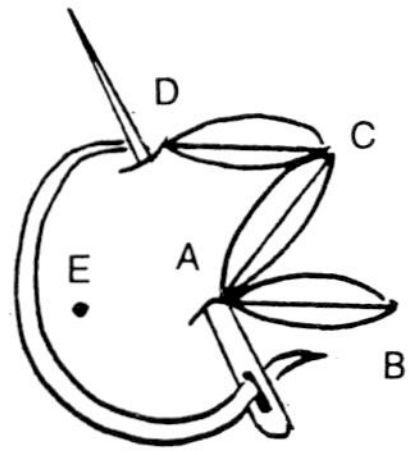

Fig. 42c

Woven Webs

Back stitch web

1. Make a double cross A-B-C-D-E-F-G-H as in Figure 43.
2. Bring needle and yarn out at the centre of the crosses.
3. Take the needle over and back one arm of the cross and forward under two arms, not through the fabric.
4. Pull the stitch with an even tension to form a back stitch over the bar.
5. Repeat in a spiral direction out to the edge of the crosses.

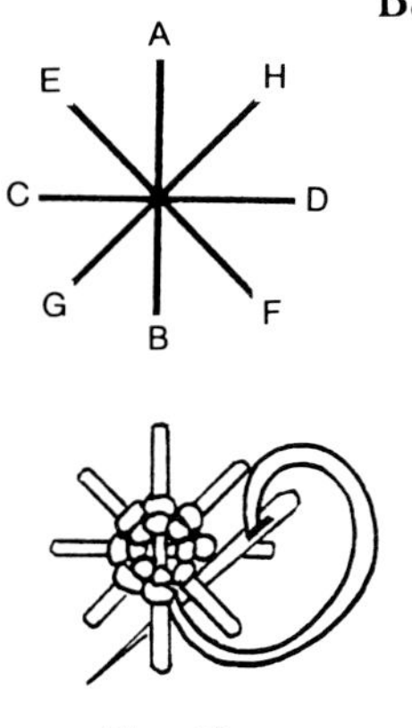

Fig. 43

Cretan stitch web

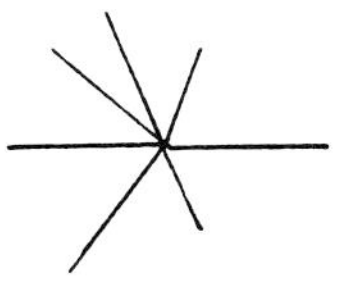

Fig. 44a

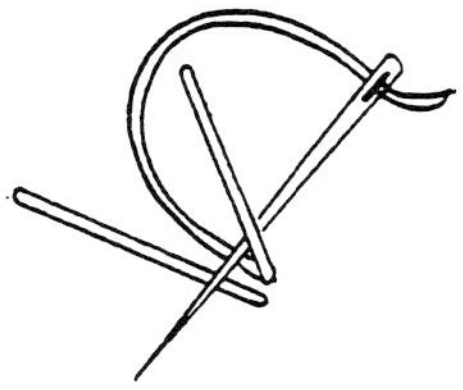

Fig. 44b

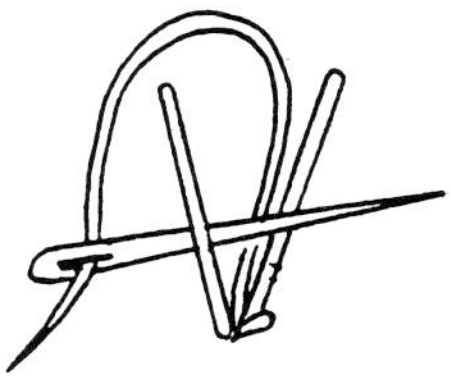

Fig. 44c

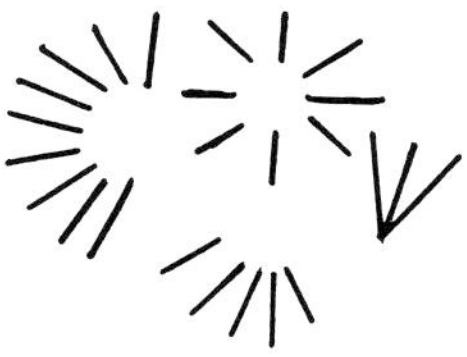

Fig. 44d

1. Work straight stitches into a central point as in Figure 44. These stitches can be evenly or unevenly spread and of different lengths.
2. Commencing at the centre of two arms work Cretan stitch between the two arms.
3. Continue working Cretan stitch between the pairs of arms until the desired effect is achieved.

Stem stitch web

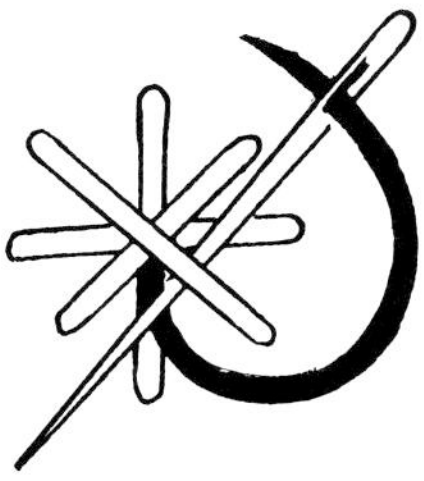

Fig. 45

1. Make a double cross A-B-C-D-E-F-G-H as in Figure 43.
2. Refer now to Figure 45 and bring needle and yarn out at the centre of the crosses, take needle back over two arms of the crosses and forward under one, not through the fabric.
3. Pull the yarn with an even tension to create a stitch over two bars.
4. Repeat in a spiral direction out to the edge of the crosses.

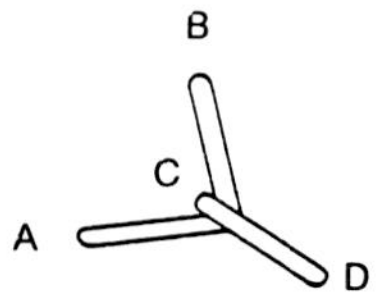

Fig. 46a

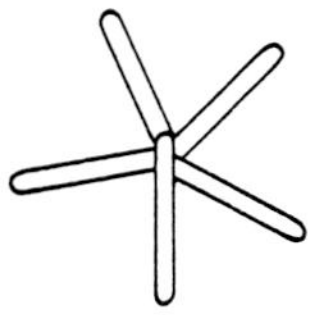

Fig. 46b

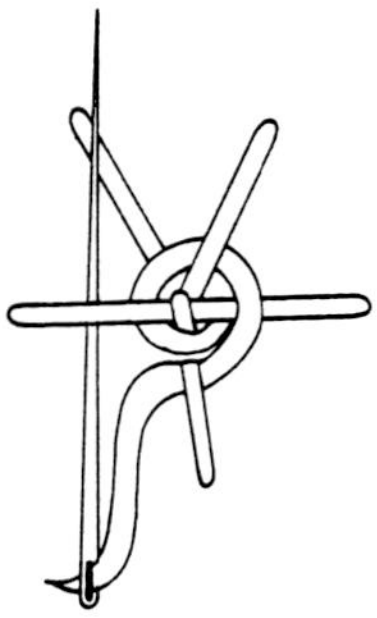

Fig. 46c

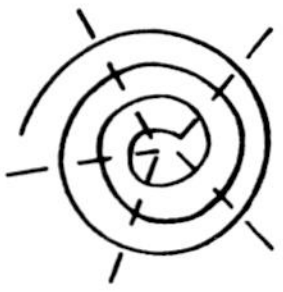

Fig. 46d

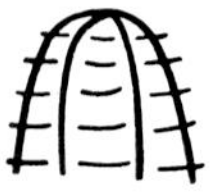

Fig. 46e

Woven web stitch - plain weave

1. Make a Y or fly stitch A-B-C-D as in Figure 46a.
2. Make two more straight stitch arms into the centre of the Y forming five arms as in Figure 46b. This web requires an uneven number of arms.
3. Bring needle and yarn out at the centre of the arms and thread needle and yarn under and over each arm in a spiral direction out to the edge with a smooth even tension resulting in a flat finish as in Figures 46c and 46d.
4. A variation of this woven web as shown in Figure 46e is to pull the thread very tightly as you weave, packing in as many spirals as possible. This results in a tight, raised mound.

General variations - All webs may be varied by weaving or stitching parts of circles. Some examples of foundation bars are illustrated in Figure 44d. Padding and foundations under the bars of the web create interesting raised effects (refer to foundations in Chapter 2).

Just the Beginning

I have had a tassel fetish, that is an irrational devotion to the tassel, for many years.

This interest was heightened in 1989 when it was my privilege to visit Wyedean Weaving in Haworth, Yorkshire, where braids, military laces, tassels and trimmings are made for military regalia, Queen's Guard, boy scouts' garter flashes, British Rail platform staff, Canadian Mounted Police, as well as Canadian and Scottish Pipers, R.A.F. and R.A.A.F. sleeve rank braid, llama braid for Eskimos and many other types of regalia. In addition to this, special orders for authentic laces, shoulders and buttonholes are made for American recreation societies for battle re-enactments. Historical works are made for films and plays. Following this visit I also spent some time at the Benaki Museum in Athens, studying the wonderful embroideries, needle made lace, fringes and tassels in the costume section. In one display in this section, a bride's outfit from Arachova included a fine woven silk scarf edged with silk fringed tassels.

Greece has a rich history of lace and fringing and fringed lace decorates doorways, windows, dresser and table covers, in addition to scarves and clothing. A common use of tasselled fringing in Greece is to hang it in the front windscreens of trucks and cars with religious medals, crucifixes and symbols to ward off 'the evil eye'.

The flower tassel in its basic form was shown to me many years ago by my late mother-in-law, Helene Mitrofanis, who learnt it in Cairo from a French lady, which illustrates the universality of the tassel.

The fuchsia tassel evolved from experiments with overskirts suggested by practical dressmaking skills. The fabric tassels are a natural progression for an avid embroiderer.

When I started making the tassels shown in this book, many new ideas kept on surfacing, suggested and evolving from experiments, projects that went wrong, or simply combining several elements which had been accidentally, or absent-mindedly, placed on a crowded table, chair or the filing system on the floor. In the same way the techniques shown in each chapter will enable you to make your own distinctive and unique tassels to add creative detail, embellishments and trims to wherever your imagination and materials will take you.

Index